SOUL & CULTURE

NUMBER NINE
Carolyn and Ernest Fay Series in Analytical Psychology
David H. Rosen, General Editor

SOUL & CULTURE

Roberto Gambini

FOREWORD BY DAVID H. ROSEN

Texas A&M University Press   *College Station*

Copyright © 2003 by Roberto Gambini
Manufactured in the United States of America
All rights reserved
First edition

The paper used in this book meets the minimum requirements
of the American National Standard for Permanence
of Paper for Printed Library Materials, z39.48-1984.
Binding materials have been chosen for durability.

∞

The photographs of newspapers in chapter 1 of this book were taken by Regina Martins. All other photographs were taken by the author.

Cover illustration: From Carl Friedrich Philipp von Martius, Tabulae Vegetationis in Brasilia physiognomian illustrantes, 1856.

Library of Congress Cataloging-in-Publication Data

Gambini, Roberto, 1944–
  Soul and culture / Roberto Gambini ; foreword by David H. Rosen.—1st ed.
    p. cm.—(Carolyn and Ernest Fay series in analytical psychology ; no. 9)
  Includes bibliographical references and index.
  ISBN 1-58544-214-3 (alk. paper)
  1. Personality and culture. 2. Psychoanalysis and culture.
  I. Title. II. Series.
BF698.9.C8G35   2003
150.19'54—dc21   2002013748

CONTENTS

Series Editor's Foreword, by David H. Rosen VII

Preface XI

1. The Collective Unconscious Comes to the Newspaper 3
2. Soul Making in the New World 37
3. Urban Trees as Mirrors of the Soul 58
4. The Alchemy of Cement in a Modern City 83
5. Bringing Soul Back to Education: Dreams in the Classroom 104

Notes 127

Bibliography 131

Index 135

NUMBER NINE
Carolyn and Ernest Fay Series in Analytical Psychology
David H. Rosen, General Editor

The Carolyn and Ernest Fay edited book series, based initially on the annual Fay Lecture Series in Analytical Psychology, was established to further the ideas of C. G. Jung among students, faculty, therapists, and other citizens and to enhance scholarly activities related to analytical psychology. The Book Series and Lecture Series address topics of importance to the individual and to society. Both series were generously endowed by Carolyn Grant Fay, the founding president of the C. G. Jung Educational Center in Houston, Texas. The series are in part a memorial to her late husband, Ernest Bel Fay. Carolyn Fay has planted a Jungian tree carrying both her name and that of her late husband, which will bear fruitful ideas and stimulate creative works from this time forward. Texas A&M University and all those who come in contact with the growing Fay Jungian tree are extremely grateful to Carolyn Grant Fay for what she has done. The holder of the McMillan Professorship in Analytical Psychology at Texas A&M functions as the general editor of the Fay Book Series.

FOREWORD

*We are not human beings having a spiritual experience;
we are spiritual beings having a human experience.*

Pierre Teilhard de Chardin

Roberto Gambini is one of those rare individuals who embodies what he is lecturing and writing about. He is an analyst for both the individual and the world. From the moment I met him, I felt a soul connection, and that is why we started and have continued to call each other "brother." Upon arriving at my home, Roberto gave me a gift: a wooden turtle handmade by the Karajá Indians of Brazil. I was touched because it is my favorite helping animal, and there are many of them in various forms around my house. How did Roberto know? He said that he just knew on a deep intuitive level. The turtle in American Indian mythology, as well as other cultures, is a symbol of the Earth or Great Mother.[1] The meaning of this animal is central to efficacious love and work. It is all about being grounded and going slow (in order to attend to everything and complete creative activities—recall the old fable of "The Tortoise and the Hare"). The turtle's two homes are water and earth, both are related to the feminine principle. Hence, the turtle also represents flowing harmoniously with one's situation, yet when necessary standing firmly on the ground for one's position, as well as exhibiting motherly compassion. The truth is that we are never alone as children or adults (culture and one human family) of the Earth (World Soul). We are a product of and always connected to the Great Mother Earth.

After Roberto's Fay Lectures were over, he wanted to go to West Texas to see Marfa, where the film *Giant* was made. The first day he was going to visit Enchanted Rock (a sacred American Indian site sort of like Ayers

Rock in Australia). Roberto drove through the park and decided not to climb to the top of the rock. As he turned to head back to Fredericksburg, he noticed something green in the road. Roberto stopped his car, got out, and picked up a live turtle off the pavement. It looked like a ceramic turtle I had made in Japan that he had seen at my home. He thought it was a sign. After letting the turtle go free in a grassy field, Roberto then returned to Enchanted Rock and made it to the top in time for the sunset. He had a moment of epiphany and peace. In memory of the event, Roberto wrote this haiku:

> *Green turtle on asphalt*
> *Unexpectedly*
> *My friend is with me*

The turtle synchronicity is the same kind of unconscious-to-conscious link that Frank McMillan III had just before his father decided to endow the first professorship in analytical (Jungian) psychology at Texas A&M University. Frank III dreamt that saplings of trees were growing up through cement. This vivid archetypal dream echoes the central theme of this book: Soul and culture (Nature and human nature), a joining of opposites. It parallels the fact that now half of the students at Texas A&M are female and the fastest growing college is Liberal Arts; historically it was all male, military, and focused primarily on agriculture and mechanics (engineering). As John Sanford said, "The soul herself, which is always feminine, must be present if healing is to occur." And healing is a process toward wholeness.

As he outlines in his preface, Roberto Gambini's book concerns five aspects of soul and culture. Five is a number of change, and change we must if we are to preserve soul and culture. His five chapters focus on the collective unconscious becoming conscious. Gambini starts in chapter 1 by investigating the front pages of the leading São Paulo newspaper, finding evidence of archetypes and the collective unconscious.

In light of the terrorist attacks on September 11, 2001, everything has changed in America and the world. Now Gambini's second chapter, "Soul Making in the New World," takes on a new and special significance. We must confront and transform evil on a world scale. We must prevent *omnicide*—what I call mass or world suicide—and focus on the whole human family based on Earthly spiritual values.[2] Jung's central archetype of the Self (*imago Dei*, Supreme Being, or Higher Force) needs to be the primary ordering principle for the individual psyche (soul), as well as for the World Soul and culture (one human family). We must have this vision if we are to transcend egoistical nations and truly become a spiritual global village grounded by an effective United Nations. We have the means to feed, clothe, shelter, and educate all members of the world living on this planet Earth. We can achieve harmony and peace. The choice is ours, but it means transforming warring nations (like individuals full of rage, hell-bent on homicide and suicide) through *nationcide* (like *egocide*) and creating an integrated and interdependent, healthy, soulful one world community.[3] In chapter 3, "Urban Trees as Mirrors of the Soul," I am again reminded of Frank McMillan III's dream, which is related to Jung's psychology being at Texas A&M University, and Gambini's giving voice to injured trees as a reflection of our injured souls. Gambini's fourth chapter, "The Alchemy of Cement in a Modern City," also relates to Frank III's dream and for the need of combining opposites, which leads to a new creation. Gambini writes insightfully about how the artist is the soulful healer of our decaying cities. The last chapter, "Bringing Soul Back to Education," is an ingenious idea about what is required in the education of our youngest children. As revealed by the children's colorful pictures and important words, the power of dreams in the classroom is a testament to the soul's natural healing force.

Roberto Gambini is a shaman-like guide, and this healing book, which contains turtle soul medicine, is a needed map for navigating through treacherous waters. The key is the crossing and arriving safely on the other shore. We can only accomplish this with great sacrifice (which means to make sacred), thereby establishing one world where everyone is secondary to a Higher Force. And let us remember the wisdom of the Talmud, which characterizes immortality as three things: (1) having a child or children; (2) planting a tree or trees; and (3) writing a book or books or creating other artistic products. This timely and timeless book will help us save our soul and culture.

—David H. Rosen

PREFACE

The great challenge of our time is the urgent need to transform the way we are used to looking at what we call "reality." It has taken centuries for our Western minds to come to an uncritical certainty that life, or the world, or reality—the name has no importance—has two dimensions: one out there, and another here inside. Object and subject have become the leading protagonists of the most dramatic stage narrative ever imagined. Facing each other, arguing with each other, combating and separating each other by means of all kinds of reasons, weapons, and convictions, both actors have endeavored throughout the centuries—at least in the Western half of the planet—to reassert themselves as completely different from their opponent, their radically different Other.

We are now entering an age in which it is no longer possible to believe that time-honored enactment. The masks are falling apart, only to reveal, to a surprised audience, that the actors are twins, even if they play contrasting roles. The number two is being superseded by the number one. All that for ages has been perceived as duality is coming to a point of no return, in which everyone begins to see that *two* is just *one* with two sides.

What a challenge for dramatists! If two is one, then out is in—and what to do with thousands of books, countless theories, widespread certainties that explained the world, reality, human life? What to do with all of that? Well, just simply let it all change! What we call "reality" seems to want *us* to change and understand it in a new way. Reality is tired of our repetitious narrowness.

What is reality requiring from us at this point in the history of consciousness? That we mature, leave behind our adolescent grandiose fantasies of knowledge, and be brave enough to look at it with new eyes and realize that reality is still more complex, more subtle, and more intelligent than we had thought so far. It wants us to recognize its ingenuity in being a concealed double mirror, not just an opaque object to be looked at, but something that reflects the very nature of the observer.[1] What reality wants is that we discover that when we are looking at it we are at the same time looking at us: humans mirror outside reality, and reality mirrors our soul. No separation, just correspondence. This idea is so ancient.

What a change in the ruling principle of collective consciousness lies ahead! It may take a long time to be assimilated, but slowly it will penetrate into old states of mind. The change is almost frightening, if we think of all the practical consequences, the necessary revisions, the enormous waste that will be generated. But there is no choice: either we advance along the road of knowledge, or we will be devoured by the logic of a reality that we failed to follow up on in all its subtlety.

Soul and culture are two sides of the same coin. In this book, I will illustrate this as simply as possible. We can no longer understand history as separate from psyche, as if it were not ruled by myths and mentalities, or as if mentalities were not shaped by concrete conditions of life. If both reflect each other, they are but two forms of the same substance.

Before I graduated as an analyst from the C. G. Jung Institute in Zurich, Switzerland, I obtained a master of arts in social sciences at the University of Chicago, in the United States. In Brazil, my home country, I had already received bachelors' degrees both in law and in sociology. The depth and openness of Jungian psychology allowed me, in due time, to bring together the extroverted approach of the social sciences— sociology, anthropology, history, law, and political science—and the introverted approach of analytical psychology, with its focus on inner realities. As I went on with my studies and researches, I gradually noted that a certain standpoint was taking shape in my attempt to understand the circumstance of humanity. Of course I was familiar with Jung's theory of the *Unus Mundus*[2] and all the intellectual associations he brought up from forgotten philosophical traditions to support it. But I had never consciously intended to work theoretically with that subject, although it has become one of the foundations of my work as an analyst. In the last twenty-five years of my research in this area, I met the unitarian world in all the topics that came to my attention.

In this book I will present five pieces tied together by this common foundation, an approach that is always inquiring about the secret bond between out there and here inside, or as I have called it, between *Soul and Culture*.

In the first chapter, entitled "The Collective Unconscious Comes to the Newspaper," I invite you to look at a collection of 1997 and 1998 front-page clippings from a popular Brazilian newspaper. Something very strange happened during that period. Leafing through the newspaper over coffee, readers could suddenly find incredible mythological images, archetypal motifs, and dream scenes that usually appear in Fellini films or art books. My chapter is an attempt to understand and explain that surprising phenomenon.

Following that, in "Soul Making in the New World," I will take you to the sixteenth century, when European consciousness found itself face to face with a completely different kind of humanity, which frightened it to the bone and triggered the immediate construction of all kinds of defenses in order not to lose its own identity. The problem is that, at the same time, our Latin American identity was being built, and this is a reality that can only be understood if we make history and analytical psychology join hands.

From that trip to the past we move to present-day São Paulo. We will walk together in different kinds of neighborhoods, looking up at trees, and trying to understand what is happening to them. Most are suffering to such an extent that it will be hard not to feel moved by them. Our question will be: what are these poor trees telling us about the state of our souls? You will find this piece of reflection under the title "Urban Trees as Mirrors of the Soul."

In the fourth chapter, called "The Alchemy of Cement in a Modern City," we will again take a walk, this time inside an ugly, dilapidated building in the old center of São Paulo, to watch and comment on an art exhibit dealing with cement, sand, debris, filth, and polluted water. It may be a bit unpleasant to your good taste, but I urge you to come along, because I want to show you how medieval alchemy—the art of transmutations—is operating today to regenerate what has decayed inside our psyche and outside in the megalopolis.

We will close our journey going back to the little benches where we sat in kindergarten. In "Bringing Soul Back to Education: Dreams in the Classroom," we will try to follow step by step the fantastic world of children's dreams, as they tell them to their teachers and colleagues. Our point of interest will be: is there no room for the unconscious at school? What happens when education and analytical psychology collaborate to achieve a higher level of understanding of these highly sophisticated beings that we call "children"?

I hope my invitation will not disappoint you, and before I close, please allow me to mention three people who are essential for *Soul and Culture*'s existence. The first is Carolyn Fay, who, with her freedom of mind, has had the inspiration to create and sponsor a series of annual lectures at Texas A&M University, thus allowing Jungian analysts from different cultures to express freely their views on a rich variety of subjects. Also, through her generosity, the Fay Book Series in Analytical Psychology was created. At this point enters David Rosen, who coordinates the Fay Lectures and edits the Fay books. He gives the speakers excellent conditions to express their deepest thoughts in an environment full of care, freedom, and friendship. In cases such as mine—I am not a native English speaker—he even takes the trouble to revise manuscripts and make sensitive corrections and suggestions. He also has enormous patience with people like me, who have certain difficulties using e-mail or delivering material on time. I also want to thank the Texas A&M University Press for understanding that my work relies heavily on images that had to be printed with the text to make it intelligible. And finally comes Fátima Salomé Gambini, with whom I shared the feelings, intuitions, ideas, and initiatives that enabled me to carry out my researches. Through her interest and receptivity, I had the courage to believe and love them.

SOUL & CULTURE

CHAPTER 1

The Collective Unconscious Comes to the Newspaper

My way of working as a Jungian, intellectually speaking, is to let myself be impressed and influenced by the place where I live, the spirit of the time, and whatever touches my soul, with the least criticism possible. It is fascinating to notice how the soul itself calls my attention from time to time and whispers in my ear: "Hey, why don't you pay closer attention to this or that; why don't you try to say something about it from my point of view?" It is very refreshing and reassuring to make this kind of commitment to listen to your soul's intention that you could apply your knowledge, your intelligence, and your equipment to shape something that is not yet in scholarly books. So I have allowed myself to skip from observing and photographing damaged trees to considering new dimensions of art works, newspapers, city planning, native Indian psychology, education and the unconscious, and so on. This is how I have been building a collection of topics.

For Jung, myth and mythical images were self-expressions of the soul. The soul would tell humanity, in each different culture and in varying moments of time, something like, "This is what life is really about; this is what we are all here for; this is what we are made of; this is where we are going." Myth is very different from science, but it can be as deep, as encompassing, and as inspiring.

If you remember, Jung used mythological comparisons to make hallucinations understandable. One of his first works was translating the unintelligible language of Babette, one of his first patients in the psychiatric hospital in Zurich, and in so doing he opened the door to the understanding of the mutterings and visions of schizophrenics or those in altered states of consciousness, having shown that bizarre, surreal, weird, unheard of contents, behaviors, words, and images can find parallels in mythological themes.

Mythology is like the water under the ground upon which we are all standing. If we connect to that mythic level, we can assess ourselves and our circumstances more deeply and see meaning in certain aspects of human life that might easily pass unnoticed. Newspapers allow us a link to the river of myths.

Newspapers are part of the media. *Medium* is a Latin word that means a vehicle to inter*mediate,* to transmit information, or to let the psyche express itself. Perhaps, deep down, what a medium does is to allow for the embodiment or incorporation of the psyche, as in mediumistic phenomena—something Jung also studied in the beginning of his career. A medium would lower ego consciousness for the purpose of giving expression to unconscious aspects of his or her personality, of groups, of culture at large, and even to transmit voices of the dead. A newspaper would then be a medium in the same sense. It could give form and body to new knowledge, new perceptions of reality, or emerging values. But we know that the media, as the fourth power in a democratic society, is not ruled exactly by that principle, but by commercial convenience and the political interests of the Establishment—a sociological term for what we call collective consciousness.

Most of us read the newspaper every morning. In a certain period of my life I refused to read the newspaper due to rebellion, excessive introversion, or sheer lack of interest and habit. It may have happened to some of you. When I see people putting their faces in front of those huge double pages I wonder what are they really doing. Are they reading the paper as they would a piece of literature, a poem, a report, a letter? Probably many different things happen when you read the newspaper. First, you can take some time for yourself. You then have a good alibi not to be disturbed, because obviously you are doing something important for your career and your status as a conscious citizen. You can legitimately put a screen in front of your face and then connect the emotions, fantasies, thoughts, and inner dialogues you are having in that moment. You can let your inner newspaper unfold, and it can be much more engaging than the touchable one: you are not reading anything really, you are only watching your inner film. Or you can do active, if not mainly passive, imagination while you look at the printed news: you can project the worst possibility of your shadow onto criminals, onto those being accused of utterly immoral deeds, or those involved in scandals, in pathological or deviant behavior. Or then you can project still unrealized potentials onto scientists, artists, pioneers, winners in general. In a newspaper one could find echoes, personalizations, and equivalents for a good part of our inner world of images, thoughts, and emotions. So there is a lot of psychic processes going on, and I think we should pay more attention to what happens while we do such a simple and commonplace act as opening a newspaper in front of our eyes—like a mirror—everyday.

In my home town I subscribe to a newspaper, a traditional and influential one called precisely *O Estado de São Paulo*. It is more than one hundred years old and almost four hundred thousand copies are printed everyday, reaching one million readers on special weekends, with nationwide distribution—and think how big Brazil is. It is something like *The New York Times*, the main difference being that it is a Third World newspaper, and that counts—but it has the same basic structure and outlook.

In mid-1997, I was perusing the paper over morning coffee, before seeing my first patient. A particular image caught my whole attention. Overwhelmed, I asked myself, "What is happening here? This is not the place for such an image. It belongs in a Jungian book, a big art book, but not on the front page of a newspaper!" So I cut out that page and kept it in a folder, not knowing whether anything else might develop. A few days later, another image called my attention in a similar way, and I decided to collect front pages such as these two and verify a hypothesis. Was something new happening here? Were archetypal images "wanting" to invade, or take over, this very conservative political space, the most influential national newspaper's front page? As my collection grew, this hypothesis seemed to hold true, and then I thought that culture, or collective consciousness, in certain moments of time *wants* to open up and make room for contents that are emerging from the collective unconscious. Seemingly, this was the ripe time for it to happen. Maybe some aspects of the unconscious were moving toward the visible surface of perception in order to be assimilated and recognized in a new way, following a necessity and a finalistic logic far beyond our full rational grasp. If there is some truth to this, an important psychic process would be taking place, and then my working hypothesis is correct: our culture is ready and intends to integrate a little bit more of its great unknown matrix, just that bit it is able to swallow in the present time. If this is really happening, we can all realize that important psychological, cultural, and social changes are on the make. We can then stimulate this process, deepen it, work on it, elaborate on it, and detect possible consequences.

We all know, after all that Jung said, that collective consciousness has to change before outward reality may change. All historical transformation—let us put it bluntly—starts at the psychic level, although social scientists still resist the idea. Before we have new images, new values, new myths, and new ways of understanding and functioning, nothing new will happen in the outside realm. No social or cultural forms will appear.

I will now present images from the front pages of a newspaper. My comments will relate to the hypothesis I mentioned. Interestingly enough, one year or so after I had started collecting these clippings, all of a sudden the same front page became dull again, with all those mind-inspiring images vanishing into the blue from where they came. I cannot explain why, from mid-1997 to mid-1998, there was this blossoming of soul images in a very conservative newspaper, which just as suddenly stopped—the visual outlook of the front page going back to what it had always been. I certainly could research that further. For instance, I could call and make an appointment with the newspaper's headquarters, talk to the front-page photograph editor of that period, and ask if they were aware of what they were doing. I could have inquired if it were a marketing experiment or a specific taste of the person in charge, who then might have been dismissed or dissuaded to go on playing with images. But I have not done it thus far. You could legitimately think that all I am and will say is nothing but the result of a person's deliberate action, and that I am just one of those Jungians who believe in what they intuit and sense, fooling themselves and the public with the vain assumption that what sounds true to them has general validity. All I can say is that I think my hypothesis is true, and that I am taking risks. Now decide for yourself. But are we in the field of rational certainties? I prefer to say that this hypothesis does good for the soul and harms no one. Recently, I was courteously given a local newspaper to read over breakfast. It was dull, like any other paper concentrating on sports, with very unimaginative images. I wonder if this particular paper has always been like that, if it will ever change or not. Now that I am engaged in this work I look for evidences everywhere—and this is the excitement of it.

In 1662, René Descartes compared the creation of memory images in the brain to the indelible traces left by needles piercing a piece of stretched-out silk fabric.[1] It is a fitting metaphor for what happens when we look at an archetypal image. The brain, like the silk tissue, is imprinted by the outer image, which then is retained in an inner "archive." In the seventeenth century the thought was already current that images definitely made an impression on the brain. They would not say "psyche," because that was the time in which rational empiricism was the great new achievement. And, nowadays, with depth psychology and neurophysiology, we know much more about that phenomenon—or do we really? It is very probable that when we look at archetypal images something of the sort happens. Something definitely powerful, to say the least, happens when we come in contact with archetypal images of any kind—nice or ugly, benevolent or destructive—we just do not know exactly what. Even if we do not pay enough attention, subliminally they reach us and affect our psyche. This is precisely our concern. To illustrate this, I have distributed my material into categories: "The World of Myth," "The Elements," "The Animal World," "The Dream World," "Power," and "The Anima."

The World of Myth

The first newspaper front page image that impressed me was a row of funerary urns belonging to a museum in Beirut (see figure 1). The museum had been closed for twenty-two years and was then reopening. That was the news. The sarcophagi on display were two thousand years old. The diagonal line in which they were pictured alluded to a receding and lost past, conveying the notion that silent witnesses of immemorial time were coming back to contact with us in the present. Looking at this photograph, side by side with very matter-of-fact news, I suddenly realized that the unique quality of this image carried away and ignited my imagination into timelessness. But the following picture, which I saw a few days later, was the crucial one, for it set me to work systematically with a clear hypothesis in mind.

A diver explores the muddy waters in which Alexandria was once submerged and is overwhelmed (look at his eyes inside the mask) when he finds himself face to face with a statue of the goddess Isis (see figure 2). Is this not a perfect image to illustrate the encounter between the male ego and the feminine anima archetype drowned for ages in the unconscious? Of course, the caption would not make allusions of this kind, but you do not have to be a Jungian to be affected immediately by the suggestive strength of such an image.

In the same week a front page featured the secretary of the treasury, violence, and a statue of Ramses being fished out of dark waters. Maybe the editor played with the idea of placing two power figures together, perhaps believing to be subtly ironic. But there is much more to it: the archetype of power reasserting its timelessness and the possibility of consciousness and the mythical unconscious coming together in a new kind of relationship.

Another front page pictured our president in front of the cross, and, below him, Spiderman in Times Square, New York. The news was that a huge balloon suddenly deflated and fell over a crowd that tried hurriedly to escape the untimely attack. The image provided a glimpse of the surprising life that quickly animated a mythic being, as if it had only pretended to be lifeless.

O ESTADO DE S. PAULO

Julio Mesquita (1891-1927) — *Julio de Mesquita Filho (1927-1969)* — ANO 118 QUINTA-FEIRA Nº 38.035 — *Francisco Mesquita (1927-1969)* — *Julio de Mesquita Neto (1969-1996)*
SÃO PAULO, 27 DE NOVEMBRO DE 1997

RUY MESQUITA
Diretor-responsável

Cemat prevê ágio pequeno hoje no leilão

O controle da empresa Centrais Elétricas Matogrossenses (Cemat) vai a leilão hoje, na Bolsa de Valores do Rio, pelo preço mínimo de R$ 323,3 milhões. Segundo o presidente da empresa, Jaconias de Aguiar, três ou quatro consórcios devem disputar o controle da companhia. "Não temos a ilusão de que consegiremos um preço 70% a 100% maior do que o mínimo, como vem ocorrendo nas privatizações de distribuidoras estaduais", disse. A Vale do Rio Doce, com a CSN e o Grupo Vicunha, pode liderar um dos grupos. **Página 83**

Novo banco dará crédito a miniprodutor

O ministro de Política Fundiária, Raul Jungmann, e o presidente do Banco Central, Gustavo Franco, anunciaram a criação do Banco da Terra, que começa a operar em janeiro. Os financiamentos para compra de terras ficarão entre R$ 10 mil e R$ 15 mil. Recursos de R$ 400 milhões dos provenientes de contas bancárias não recadastradas. Verba de R$ 1,3 milhão será liberada para custear lavouras e assentar 150 famílias em São Paulo. Terminou ontem protesto de sem-terra na sede do Incra na capital. **Página A12**

500 produtos poderão ter alíquota menor

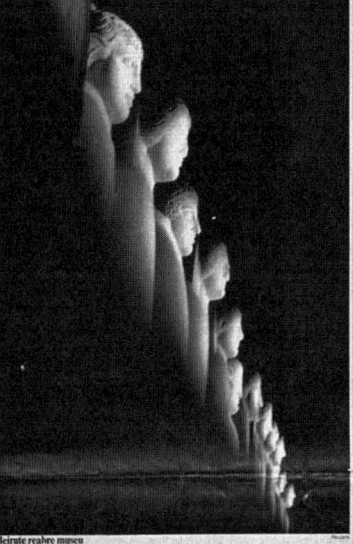

O governo iniciou a identificação de equipamentos que poderão ser importados com tarifas reduzidas. Eles não são similar nacional nem no Mercosul. A lista, de cerca de 500 itens, substituirá quase 4 mil bens de capital que entravam no País sem imposto porque estavam incluídos num regime especial revogado em julho. Com o ajuste fiscal, a alíquota passou de 17% para 20%. Se a lista for aprovada pelo Mercosul, os produtos poderão entrar em toda a região com tarifas entre 5% e 7%, segundo os técnicos. **Página 89**

NOTAS E INFORMAÇÕES
O Brasil continuará a ser um bom lugar para investir, segundo o presidente, porque está longe da saturação dos mercados e porque suas instituições são seguras. Essas é a mensagem correta. **"O que FHC espera da crise", em página 83**

TEMPO
SUAS CONTAS
HOJE 142 páginas
Classificados 12.568 ofertas

Beirute reabre museu
Coleção de sarcófagos do quinto século antes de Cristo pode ser vista novamente no Museu Nacional de Beirute, reaberto depois de 22 anos de fechamento e um programa de reconstrução que custou US$ 3 milhões. Durante a guerra civil, entre 1975 e 1990, o museu foi usado como ponto para esconderijos por franco-atiradores. **Página A14**

Brinquedo proibido
Carro no computador avança para "atear" pedestre, jogo que o governo quer banir **Página C3**

Santos goleia Internacional e Portuguesa perde do Vasco

O Santos goleou o Internacional por 4 a 0, ontem à noite, no Morumbi, e manteve a esperança de ir para a final do Campeonato Brasileiro. Os gols foram de Alexandre, Müller, Marcos Assunção e Caíco. A equipe santista, porém, ficará desfalcada de pelo menos cinco titulares contra o próprio Inter, sábado, em Porto Alegre, já pelo segundo turno da fase semifinal. A Portuguesa caiu diante do Vasco por 2 a 1, depois de ter saído em vantagem, no Rio. O artilheiro do campeonato, Edmundo, marcou o gol da vitória. O atacante Paulo Nunes, que defendeu o Grêmio, foi contratado ao Benfica pelo Parmalat e poderá defender o Palmeiras. O São Paulo disputa hoje, em Santiago do Chile, a vaga de finalista da Supercopa dos Campeões da Libertadores. A partida, às 22h20 de Brasília, terá transmissão pela TV Bandeirantes e o time brasileiro pode até perder por 1 a 0 para alcançar a classificação.

Deputados derrubam estabilidade de servidor

Planalto obtém 326 votos na batalha mais significativa da reforma administrativa

A Câmara aprovou ontem em segundo turno a quebra da estabilidade dos servidores, que poderão ser demitidos para contenção de gastos. O Planalto venceu sua batalha mais significativa na votação da reforma administrativa por 326 votos a favor, 154 contra e 2 abstenções. Em seu esforço, o governo pediu apoio até ao presidente do PPB, Paulo Maluf. O presidente Fernando Henrique Cardoso telefonou para cada um dos deputados vistos como problemáticos. "O presidente nunca entrou tão firme numa votação", disse o líder do PFL, Inocêncio Oliveira (PE), satisfeito com a mudança de posição de quatro parlamentares conseguida por FHC. A emenda permitirá aos Estados e municípios que demitam funcionários sempre que os gastos com pessoal ultrapassarem 60% da receita. O texto ainda será votado pelo Senado. Outra vitória de FHC foi a recusada de um destaque que abria exceções no novo teto salarial de R$ 12,7 mil para o funcionalismo. Já aprovado na reforma. Com ajuda da oposição, o governo conseguiu eliminar a possibilidade de gratificações e vantagens pessoais ficarem fora do novo teto. **Página A4**

Bolsa de Tóquio reage e países discutirão crise

A Bolsa de Tóquio fechou ontem em alta de 1,2%, numa demonstração de confiança do mercado financeiro japonês no governo, apesar da confirmação da quebra de outro banco, o Tokuyo City. A tensão quanto ao futuro do sistema bancário do Japão, porém, não foi afastada. Essa crise fez crescer a responsabilidade do Fórum de Cooperação Econômica da Ásia e do Pacífico, que reuniria ministros das Finanças de países da região e de potências de outros continentes, na próxima semana, em Kuala Lumpur, na Malásia. O encontro discutirá fórmulas para estabilizar o mercado financeiro global e evitar novas crises. A Bolsa de São Paulo teve alta de 2,42%. **Páginas B12 e B13**

Toyota mantém investimento e Michelin anuncia planos

A Toyota manterá o investimento inicial de US$ 400 milhões e não mudará seu programa para a produção de veículos em País, por acreditar que as medidas do ajuste fiscal serão temporárias. O superintendente da montadora, Shoji Shima, diz que explicará à matriz, no Japão, em janeiro, detalhes do plano do governo, mas está otimista quanto à possibilidade de retomada do crescimento. O grupo francês Michelin também demonstra confiança no Brasil e estuda a instalação de uma fábrica de pneus no País. A Siemens, da Alemanha, confirma investimento de US$ 55 milhões em 98, completado US$ 100 milhões no biênio 97/98. A empresa alemã Ehring Klinger inaugura hoje fábrica em Piracicaba, com investimento de R$ 2,4 milhões. **Páginas B13, B21 e B28**

Aprovado novo Código Civil

O Senado aprovou o novo Código Civil, em tramitação há mais de 20 anos, que muda em grande para herança e adoção. Entre as novidades estão a redução da idade para maioridade, de 21 para 18 anos, e o fim da distinção entre filhos legítimos e ilegítimos. O texto terá de voltar para a Câmara. **Página A14**

Taxa de desemprego é a maior desde 85 **Página B1**
Governo cobrará mais impostos dos bancos **Página B1**
USP será aberta para visitas culturais **Página C1**
Segundo Ipea, guerra fiscal causa prejuízo **Página B7**
Telesp libera ações a partir do dia 10 **Página B15**
Carros de placas 7 e 8 estão no rodízio hoje

Coleção Videomagia Estadão
Próximo domingo, "Príncipe Valente"

Mergulhador atrás da deusa Ísis, protetora dos faraós: peça foi descoberta em parte da cidade submersa, ao lado de Alexandria

FIGURE 2

In the next example, the subtitle indicates that city officials are not efficient and careful enough to have public statues properly cleaned from time to time (see figure 3). But the surreal image of bees coming out of hollowed eyes immediately transports the viewer to the world of archetypal imagination, fairy tales, poetry, and art. The contrast is shocking: above, you read "Interest rates go down," then there is a bridge and a church. But the focus of attention is the Dali-like, other-worldly vision used to illustrate a rather irrelevant piece of information. Do bees spring forward from the innermost of our minds, through the holes of our eyes, when we face the gods? Or do they send their bees to provoke us?

Another newspaper cover grouped a soccer player, our green and yellow flag, racing cars, and a mythological monster left behind somewhere after Rio's Carnival parade was over. The great Dionysian festivity lasting for days has come to an end, but an imaginary beast insists to stay with us in our daily state of mind. Is that not precisely what happens in the psyche? Bugs and beasts and monsters can come to us at any time, regardless of official dates when they are allowed to run free.

O ESTADO DE S. PAULO

RUY MESQUITA
Diretor-responsável

Julio Mesquita (1891-1927) — *Julio de Mesquita Filho (1927-1969)* — ANO 119 Nº 38.135 TERÇA-FEIRA SÃO PAULO, 17 DE MARÇO DE 1998 — *Francisco Mesquita (1927-1969)* — *Julio de Mesquita Neto (1969-1996)*

Queda de juros chega ao consumidor

ANP age para conter fraude na gasolina

A Agência Nacional do Petróleo (ANP) decidiu suspender temporariamente todas as concessões a novas distribuidoras de combustíveis. O diretor-geral da ANP, David Zylbersztajn, explicou que a suspensão faz parte do combate às fraudes. Uma das preocupações da ANP é com o aumento de 1.300% na importação de solventes nos últimos meses, evidenciando a mistura deste produto à gasolina, com risco de desgaste prematuro de veículos. A fiscalização nos postos será reforçada. **Pág. 83**

Governo libera preço do gás em SP e no Rio

O preço do gás de cozinha está liberado em São Paulo e no Rio, a partir de hoje, mas o governo pretende fiscalizar 290 pontos de revenda para evitar abusos, segundo o Ministério da Fazenda, que admite a possibilidade de reajuste nesses Estados. Nas demais regiões do País, os preços continuam controlados, porem agora com aumento médio de 10,4%, tornando o botijão de 13 quilos de Gás Liquefeito de Petróleo (GLP) mais caro R$ 0,77. **Pág. 85**

Pesquisa mostra que as taxas começam a cair em todas as linhas de crédito pessoal dos bancos

A redução de juros determinada pelo Banco Central para o mercado financeiro começa a chegar ao consumidor. Pesquisa do Procon-SP mostra que a taxa média para o crédito pessoal em rede bancária caiu 0,41 ponto percentual na primeira quinzena de março – de 6,79% para 6,38% ao mês. Em termos anuais, a redução foi de 9,92 pontos, mas os juros cobrados ainda são considerados estratosféricos – 110% ao ano – para uma economia com inflação perto de zero. As reduções mais acentuadas ocorreram nas linhas de empréstimo pessoal, aquelas nas quais não se exige informação sobre a finalidade do crédito. O Banco Real, por exemplo, baixou sua taxa mensal de 7,5% para 4,5% ao mês. O Bandeirantes, de 6% para 5% e o Mercantil, de 7,4% para 6,7%. Na taxa média para o cheque especial, houve a ligeira redução, de 11,21% para 11,14% ao mês. No mercado financeiro, a TBC está fixada em 28% ao ano. No início de 98, quando o BC começou a reduzir as taxas para o mercado, previa-se que o reflexo dessa medida demoraria a chegar ao consumidor, por causa do alto nível de inadimplência. A queda dos juros para o crédito pessoal, porém, já ocorre em todas as linhas e em praticamente todos os bancos, como mostra a pesquisa. **Pág. 81**

Marca do abandono – Abelhas saem pelos olhos da estátua "O Semeador", dentro da qual mantêm uma colmeia; a escultura, na Praça Apecatu, perto do Ceagesp, no Vila Leopoldina, está suja, com a base pichada e rodeada de mato, a exemplo de várias outras de São Paulo. **Pág. C3**

TAM reduz as tarifas para mais duas rotas
Pág. B8

Cesta básica sobe e já supera salário mínimo
Pág. B6

Juíza carioca apóia discriminação da maconha e cocaína **Pág. A13**

Prazo para corte de gasto com pessoal deve ser prorrogado **Pág. A4**

Senado e Câmara disputam projeto sobre imunidade **Pág. A5**

BID vai dobrar o financiamento para empresas brasileiras **Pág. B6**

500 pessoas seguem com chuva enterro de Tim Maia no Rio **Pág. A10**

VIAGEM

Côte d'Azur é charme, sol e badalação

Treze cidades formam a Côte d'Azur, uma das mais charmosas e badaladas regiões de toda a Europa. Banhada pelo azul-celeste do Mar Mediterrâneo, esse pedaço privilegiado da França, disputadíssimo pelos turistas, tem em Nice e Cannes – sede do festival de cinema – seus pontos mais conhecidos. **Viagem**

NOTAS E INFORMAÇÕES

Se o governo brasileiro está mesmo empenhado em duplicar o valor das exportações do País, deveria eliminar os entraves a que se submetem os pequenos exportadores. Não bastam as iniciativas isoladas. "O rico filão do comércio virtual", na pág. A3

Seca – Rio Mucajaí, perto de Boa Vista, quase seco, reflete a estiagem que afeta Roraima, atingido por grandes incêndios **Pág. A12**

Últimos retoques – Operários trabalham na restauração do Teatro São Pedro, na Barra Funda **Pág. C8**

FMI defende maior liberação do comércio **Pág. B6**

Clinton rebate nova acusação de assédio **Pág. A16**

PF apura denúncia de desvio de papéis por Naya **Pág. C5**

Desculpas do Vaticano não contentam judeus **Pág. A14**

Moacyr Luz lança o samba do mandingueiro **Pág. D1**

Sai hoje decisão sobre futuro da Mancha Verde **Pág. E1**

Coleção Castelo Rá-Tim-Bum Estadão

FIGURE 3

The Elements

First we have a picture of Jupiter taken from a satellite (see figure 4), alongside a scene of violence and Pinochet, the Chilean dictator who was trying to escape judgment for the atrocities he committed. The remote planet's intriguing texture is what catches the eye—one cannot figure out at once if it is a road system, or some high-tech fabric, or some kind of animal hide seen through a zoom lens. Then you realize that you never laid your eyes on that distant body before. This is the first time. The next probable association is with unlimited space, celestial bodies in eternal rotation, the dance of the spheres, cosmological order, and, why not, the fantasy of extra-terrestrial life, ETs, aliens—for just a few seconds. Then we come back to old, dark, saturnine Pinochet.

I found a similar case in a page displaying a satellite shot of the Amazon basin all dotted with red points indicating forest devastation by arson fire. We could think of technology: "How good that now we have satellites to tell us unmistakably what is really happening down here." But this dramatic and very modern image could also take us directly to the medieval notion of the all-seeing eye of God. Christian education has for centuries taught every child, in a period when imagination is getting organized, that whatever happens in this world, however big or small—a dead leaf falling from a tree, your thinking dirty thoughts—is witnessed by the omnipresent and omniscient eye of God. Satellites and their potent cameras—and this was not part of the technological blueprint—have become the modern equivalent of that transcendental eye, because they keep watch over the whole world and especially Earth, scanning every square mile of its surface, bringing to our vision scenes that we cannot see from our ground perspective. Images such as this, or the prior one, are archetypal and psychologically powerful. They put us in God's place, enabling us to see the creation from his perspective. Satellites look at us as God once did or still does. And then we are very close to the central ethical question: because we did what is photographed, and we can see it, who is responsible?

Consider the front-page grouping of a rock singer, the subject of the public deficit, and the information that fifty million people in

O ESTADO DE S. PAULO

QUARTA-FEIRA, SÃO PAULO, 11 DE MARÇO DE 1998

Privatizada, Vale alcança lucro recorde

Ajustes após a venda da empresa começaram com a demissão de 4.618 funcionários e incluíram a renegociação de investimentos não rentáveis, determinados por interesses políticos

No primeiro ano de privatização, a Companhia Vale do Rio Doce apurou, em 1997, o maior lucro já registrado em meio século de existência. O lucro bruto somou R$ 1,149 bilhão, 30,5% mais do que os R$ 799 milhões de 1996, quando a empresa ainda era estatal. Deduzidos os impostos, o lucro líquido cresceu 46% em relação ao resultado de 1996, chegando a R$ 756 milhões, dos quais a Vale pagará um total de R$ 515,4 milhões em dividendos, ou R$ 1,33 por ação ordinária ou preferencial. O pagamento de dividendos, assim, dobrou em relação a 1996, quando seu maior acionista, a União, se credenciou a receber somente R$ 0,66 por ação. O resultado financeiro da Vale surpreendeu o mercado, que esperava um resultado bruto pouco superior a R$ 700 milhões. Se a lucro de 1997 se repetir nos próximos quatro anos, os controladores privados da Vale terão de volta todo o capital investido na compra da empresa. Entre os fatores que contribuíram para o resultado, a direção da Vale destacou a desvalorização do real em relação ao dólar, que variou 7,3% entre janeiro e dezembro de 1997. A receita bruta atingiu cerca de R$ 3,2 bilhões no ano passado, 11% mais do que obtido no período anterior, chegando perto do valor da venda do controle da empresa. Depois da privatização, a direção da Vale fez ajustes na companhia, que incluíram com 4.618 demissões. Renegociou contratos com fornecedores e efetivos investimentos considerados não rentáveis e negociados com base em interesses políticos regionais, quando a empresa era estatal. **Pág. B4**

Protestos em Santiago
Policiais reprimem com jatos de água manifestação oposicionista nas ruas da capital chilena

Atos marcam saída de Pinochet

Lágrimas
Pinochet chora durante sua passagem para a reserva

LOURIVAL SANT'ANNA
Santiago

Entrou ontem para a reserva o militar há mais tempo na ativa no mundo, o ex-ditador chileno Augusto Pinochet. Depois de 65 anos a serviço do Exército, Pinochet entregou o cargo de comandante-chefe ao general Ricardo Izurieta, tudo de acordo com regras da Constituição de seu tempo de poder. Na cerimônia, houve aplausos para o ex-militar e novos senadores. Nas ruas de Santiago, ocorreram protestos contra a permanência de Pinochet, aos 82 anos, na vida pública do Chile. **Pág. A14**

Juiz decreta indisponíveis bens da Gallus

A Justiça Federal em São Paulo decretou liminarmente a indisponibilidade dos bens da Gallus Agropecuária e de seus dois sócios, Gebon Camargo dos Santos e Marli da Silva Salgado. A empresa captava dinheiro de investidores prometendo rendimentos atrativos, mas muitos se sentiram lesados e encaminharam queixas à Comissão de Valores Mobiliários. Em 30 dias, o procurador da República André de Carvalho Ramos entrará com ação civil pública para obrigar a Gallus a prestar contas de suas operações. **Pág. B9**

NOTAS E INFORMAÇÕES

O chanceler Lampreia deverá verificar, em Buenos Aires, os problemas enfrentados pelo Mercosul, antes de embarcar para Washington, onde deverá discutir importantes detalhes para a formação da Alca. "Os obvios dentro do Mercosul", na pág. A3

FHC declara "guerra ao desemprego"

O presidente Fernando Henrique Cardoso comentou ontem as ações do governo para combater o desemprego no País. Ele explicou que essas medidas, entre as quais o aperfeiçoamento dos programas de qualificação e treinamento da mão-de-obra, serão discutidas na primeira reunião ministerial do ano, sexta-feira. "E para declarar guerra ao desemprego que reúno minha equipe de governo", disse o presidente. Ontem, FHC esteve com sito ministros para preparar o encontro com os demais assessores e afirmou que todos estarão tensa hora. O presidente concluiu que o governo, sozinho, não superará o problema. **Pág. B1**

170 motoristas devem ter a carta suspensa

O Detran começa a notificar 170 motoristas que cometeram infrações gravíssimas - sem necessariamente ter atingido os 20 pontos mínimos - e podem ser os primeiros a ter a carteira de habilitação suspensa, de acordo com o novo Código de Trânsito, em vigor há 22 de janeiro. A maioria é formada por motociclistas sem capacete (60%), seguida de motoristas embriagados (30%) ou que conduziam perigosamente (10%). Pelo novo código, o motorista pode ter a carteira suspensa por dois motivos: faltas gravíssimas ou acúmulo de 20 pontos em infrações. Só depois de 22 de maio é que será definido o tempo de duração da punição. **Pág. C1**

THE WALL STREET JOURNAL AMERICAS
Crise na Indonésia agrava-se

BORGUK E SOLOMON
Jacarta

O presidente Suharto, de 76 anos, foi reeleito ontem para o sétimo mandato de cinco anos na Indonésia. A crise econômica continua viva nesse país asiático e piorou depois que quatro dos seis filhos de Suharto atacaram o FMI por intromissão em assuntos indonésios. O embaixador norte-americano faltou à cerimônia de juramento de Suharto, fato notado pela diplomacia de Jacarta. **Pág. B8**
O Estado para a publicar também in quarta-feiras o W. S. Journal Americas

Mistérios de Júpiter

Foto da Nasa mostra um sistema de estrias e fendas na superfície de Europa, lua de Júpiter. A paisagem é um desafio para os cientistas, que tentam desvendar suas origens. Um brilho branco generalizado pode ser sinal de geada. Os pontos negros ao lado das estrias paralelas indicariam gelo originário de um oceano abaixo da superfície do satélite.

O pesadelo da moradia
*Milhares esperam na fila da casa própria da CDHU, em Itapecerica da Serra; os interessados começaram a chegar na madrugada e à tarde muitos ainda não tinham sido atendidos. **Pág. C6***

Começam este ano obras da 2.ª pista da Imigrantes **Pág. C6**
Aumenta a disputa de preços na Ponte Aérea **Pág. B6**
PT e MST divergem sobre madeireiras **Pág. A11**
Tim Maia continua em coma no hospital **Pág. A12**
Palmeiras é derrotado e São Paulo goleia por 5 a 0
Zagallo chama Zé Elias e Raí é confirmado **Pág. E2**

Coleção Castelo Rá-Tim-Bum Estadão.

FIGURE 4

Northern South America will be able to watch the millennium's last eclipse of the sun. Mankind has been staring at the sun's image for thousands of years, since the dawning of culture and consciousness. The sun is one of the first symbols conceived by man to convey the source of life, of light, power, divinity, sacredness, numinosity, of consciousness itself, painted and sculpted in rocks all over the planet. Eclipses have always been dreadful episodes, due to the anxiety they created about the eventual return of light and normalcy. So here we are faced, on the front page, with an image that could be found on the back wall of a cave. We are unconsciously thrown back to archaic religious reverence for the sun god. For a split second, we share the mind of our Zoroastrian, Mithraic, Aztec, or Tupi predecessors. And then we go to work.

Water and wind also make their appearance. What is the point of newspaper photograph of a boat competition? Wind, sails, water. Regardless of whatever is written under the image, the page establishes a subliminal connection between the viewer and the elements.

Fire and water have occupied the imaginings of many astrologers and alchemists in medieval times in their efforts to understand how opposing qualities can destroy each other or produce something new, if they only collaborate and integrate. An image of fire, not in the fireplace but let loose in a forest, conveys immediately the feeling of uncontrollable danger, destruction, and devastation. It is a dormant feeling, because if it were closer to the conscious mind, a national outcry would move politicians to do something to curb this tragic situation. A ship approaching disturbingly close to a shore, where a couple quietly rests on an easy chair (see figure 5), puts us in a Fellini atmosphere, or in a dream far away from routine. Another day, readers could view the Rio airport on fire. Behind the news, we have the ancient fight of the elements, fire, earth and air, and not enough water, reminding us that concrete solidity may become suddenly vulnerable and that even the utmost technology is not beyond the powers of nature.

The last image of this series is a fantastic rainbow (see figure 6). Our country, like many others in the Third World, has deep, cruel social problems: thirty million people living in misery, disproportionate concentration of wealth in the hands of five percent of the population, corruption, underdevelopment, malnutrition, unemployment, poor

O ESTADO DE S. PAULO

EDIÇÃO SÃO PAULO

RUY MESQUITA
Diretor-responsável

Julio Mesquita (1891-1927)   Julio de Mesquita Filho (1927-1969)   ANO 119   QUINTA-FEIRA   Nº 38.137   SÃO PAULO, 19 DE MARÇO DE 1998   Francisco Mesquita (1927-1969)   Julio de Mesquita Neto (1969-1996)

Nunca entraram tantos dólares no País

De 1.º de janeiro até agora, economia brasileira recebeu US$ 11,1 bi; mais dinheiro está a caminho

Malan aceita diálogo e MST deixa prédios

O ministro da Fazenda, Pedro Malan, deve receber hoje uma comissão de deputados para tratar das invasões do MST. Os militantes do movimento que na terça-feira ocuparam prédios públicos em 16 capitais começaram a deixar os edifícios. Malan disse que a negociação só será iniciada quando todos os prédios estiverem livres. Em São Paulo, a delegacia do Ministério da Fazenda foi liberada à noite. No mesmo instante se mantinham negociações em outros Estados. **Pág. A13**

Lucro recorde do Banespa faz ação subir 25%

As ações do Banespa subiram 25,6% na Bolsa de Valores de São Paulo, ontem, um dia depois de o banco ter anunciado balanço com lucro recorde de R$ 2,037 bilhões. Foram registrados 749 negócios com ações do Banespa, que fecharam a papela a R$ 59,00 por lote de mil, a maior valorização do Ibovespa, índice composto pelas 51 papéis mais negociados no dia. Por precaução, os negócios com o banco foram iniciados às 14 horas, interrompendo a suspensão ocorrida na véspera. **Pág. B11**

EUA admitem acordo sobre aço do Brasil

Os Estados Unidos decidiram rever as barreiras impostas às exportações de aço do Brasil, na tentativa de acabar com um atrito que se impuseste entre os dois países. O secretário de Comércio dos EUA, William Daley, disse ao Estado ontem, em San José da Costa Rica, antes do encontro de ministros das Américas, que houve grande evolução no assunto. O Brasil tinha ameaçado levar o caso à Organização Mundial do Comércio. **Pág. B10**

NOTAS E INFORMAÇÕES

O governo federal viu a invasão de prédios do Ministério da Fazenda e do Incra por milhares de militantes do MST, em várias capitais, como "ato eleitoral". Infelizmente, na verdade, não se tratou disso. *"Ato revolucionário"*, em pág. A3

Fogo na Amazônia – Helicóptero que conduz o governador de Roraima, Neudo Campos, e o secretário de Políticas Regionais, Fernando Catão, sobrevoa floresta do Estado tomada por incêndios; Catão considera insuficiente ajuda da União para o perigo. **Pág. A14**

Cerca de US$ 11,1 bilhões entraram na economia brasileira nos primeiros 2 meses e 17 dias deste ano. Esse é o saldo dos ingressos e saídas de capital estrangeiro no País, um valor nunca antes alcançado em período tão curto. Em todo o ano passado, o Brasil obteve um saldo líquido de US$ 14,94 bilhões. E mais dinheiro está a caminho, estima-se no mercado financeiro que o resultado líquido de março vá ficar entre US$ 6,5 bilhões e US$ 8 bilhões. A entrada de dólares indica que as medidas tomadas após a crise asiática surtiram efeito. Ao dobrar os juros e fixá-los em um dos níveis mais altos do mundo, o BC convenceu os investidores de que o País tinha armas para conter as ondas da crise. Mas a revoada de capital externo atrás de remuneração sugere que a queda do custo do dinheiro pode ser mais rápida do que se esperava. Outro recorde pode ser batido no fim de março, quando as reservas devem atingir US$ 65 bilhões. Para controlar a ingresso de recursos, o BC quer estabelecer prazos ou percentuais mínimos para aplicações em títulos cambiais. **Págs. B1 e B2**

Temer identifica um voto "fantasma" na Previdência

O presidente da Câmara, Michel Temer (PMDB-SP), identificou um deputado que teria fraudado a votação de ontem da Previdência, registrando voto com a senha de Valdomiro Meger (PFL-PR), que estava em Maringá. O placar do plenário da Câmara registrou, por pelo menos três vezes, o voto do paranaense. "É mais um caso de falta de decoro", afirmou Temer. **Pág. A5**

Naya alega erro de cálculo no prédio que caiu

O deputado Sérgio Naya disse em depoimento à Câmara que o desabamento do Edifício Palace 2 não foi consequência do concreto e sim um erro de cálculo em dois pilares, construído por outra empresa. Mas foram encontrados cavacos de madeira e pedaços de plástico. **Pág. C1**

Ensino privado se fortalece na Alemanha

A Alemanha vive uma onda de pioneirismo em universidades privadas. O governo estadual de Baden-Württemberg autorizou a criação de duas escolas particulares. Em Stuttgart, deve ser criado um instituto de tecnologia sustentado por empresas. **Pág. A14**

KATIA ZERO
Nova York mistura culinárias

Ordem e progresso são duas coisas que devem ser ignoradas em Manhattan. Tome o exemplo da fusion, uma tendência na culinária. **Pág. D14**

Pitta troca secretários e corteja liderança do PFL — Págs. a e C6
Atletas cubanos fogem e desaparecem no mar — Pág. A17
Passe do goleiro Rivaldo é vendido ao Fluminense — Pág. E3
Queda de tarifas em Santos ajuda exportação — Pág. B3
Índia admite interesse em fabricar bomba atômica — Pág. A15
Diretor brasileiro leva Shakespeare aos EUA — Pág. D1

Encalhado – O barco panamenho Hind fica preso num banco de areia, perto de uma praia de Fort Lauderdale, na Flórida; um casal observa o navio, que não sofreu danos e nem poluiu o mar da região

Mogi Mirim goleia Palmeiras e Santos ganha de virada — Pág. E1
Previdência recebe de volta dólares levados pela fraude — Pág. A9
Planeta pode perder dois terços da água até o ano 2025 — Pág. A14

COLEÇÃO SUPERTÍTULOS
SIDNEY SHELDON
AMANHÃ, 20/3, A OUTRA FACE.

COMPRE O ESTADO E COM MAIS R$ 3,50 LEVE O BEST-SELLER.

FIGURE 5

O ESTADO DE S. PAULO

QUARTA-FEIRA, SÃO PAULO, 18 DE FEVEREIRO DE 1998

Déficit externo em janeiro foi de US$ 2,13 bi

Nos últimos 12 meses, as transações correntes do Brasil com outros países tiveram um resultado negativo de US$ 33,84 bilhões, ou 4,1% do PIB

O déficit das contas externas do Brasil voltou a aumentar em janeiro, chegando a US$ 2,13 bilhões, depois da melhora em dezembro, quando foi de US$ 1,7 bilhão. Segundo dados divulgados ontem pelo Banco Central, as contas correntes do País, que incluem as transações comerciais mais serviços, fecharam os últimos 12 meses encerrados em janeiro com resultado negativo de US$ 33,84 bilhões, equivalente a 4,18% do Produto Interno Bruto (PIB). Em janeiro, apesar da elevação do déficit, as reservas externas cresceram US$ 1,1 bilhão, atingindo US$ 33,1 bilhões, no conceito de liquidez internacional. Isso só ocorreu porque o BC anunciou mercado intervir com ouro US$ 857 milhões em títulos líquidos. Em 1997, o Brasil não conseguiu financiar integralmente o seu déficit em transações correntes e precisou usar parte das reservas. No fim do ano passado, as reservas estavam em US$ 52,2 bilhões. **Pág. B1**

Momento de trégua
Arco-íris domina a paisagem do centro do Rio, em que o Aeroporto Santos Dumont aparece ao fundo; o fenômeno ocorreu ontem, depois de uma chuva forte que provocou novas inundações em quase toda a cidade, às vésperas do carnaval. **Pág. C4**

PIB aumentou 3% em 97, segundo o IBGE

A economia brasileira cresceu no ano passado 3,03%, resultado inferior à previsão inicial do governo federal, de que a evolução atingiria entre 4% e 5%, porém superior aos 2,88% de 96. Os dados sobre o PIB, divulgados ontem pelo IBGE, ao fechar as contas do quarto trimestre, ainda são preliminares e anunciam uma revisão por capita anual de R$ 6.482,52, o correspondente a US$ 5.020,00. A produção da economia alcançou R$ 862.420 bilhões, ou US$ 806.651 bilhões, e indica a possibilidade de o Brasil integrar, já no início do próximo milênio, o grupo de países com PIB superior a US$ 1 trilhão. Apenas seis nações integram essa lista. O coordenador do PIB trimestral do IBGE, Roberto Luiz Olinto Ramos, disse que a economia brasileira não chegou a sofrer com intensidade, nos últimos meses de 97, os efeitos do pacote fiscal. Ele prevê para este trimestre maior influência das mudanças. **Pág. B1**

Aprovada a ida de Annan a Bagdá pela paz

Os cinco membros permanentes do Conselho de Segurança aprovaram ontem a viagem do secretário-geral da ONU, Kofi Annan, para Bagdá, como tentativa de buscar uma saída diplomática para a crise do Iraque. O ditador Saddam Hussein está repetindo esquema que usou na guerra de 91 para evitar ataques aliados: aparece de surpresa para dormir a cada noite numa diferente casa de família. **Págs. A14 e A15**

Audiência com Light suspensa por falta de luz

Duas interrupções no fornecimento de energia suspenderam por quase dez minutos a audiência convocada pela Agência Nacional de Energia Elétrica (Aneel), no Rio, para que a Light prestasse contas sobre a qualidade dos seus serviços. No auditório, parte dos 500 presentes pediu a cassação da concessão da empresa. Segundo a Light, os cortes foram causados por queda de árvores durante um temporal. **Pág. B5**

FHC lança as metas para o novo mandato

O governo e os empresários brasileiros precisam dispor-se a aprender a usar na lista de Zegallo para a França, o atacante evita prosseguir a polêmica com Pelé. **Pág. A3**

Contran cria selo para vistoria

O Contran decidiu criar um selo para comprovar a inspeção de segurança nos veículos e acabar com o licenciamento. O adesivo passa a valer em 60 dias, quando devem estar definidas as regras para a vistoria anual. O Contran também exigirá apenas capacete como parte obrigatória do vestuário dos motociclistas e recomendará ao público de televisão que o uso do cinto de tórax baixos, durante o tráfego, nas rodovias. **Pág. C1**

Trânsito pára na Marginal após acidente

A Marginal do Tietê teve, ontem cedo, congestionamento de mais de 18 km, por causa da redução de velocidade provocada por motoristas que queriam ver as conseqüências do acidente, no qual uma mulher morreu atropelada. Com a reflexão, a cidade bateu recorde de lentidão do trânsito matutino no ano: 96 km. **Pág. C2** No metrô, a linha da Paulista parou ontem duas vezes, por falta de energia. **Pág. C4**

ONGs querem conter corte de matas no Brasil

O Grupo de Trabalho Amazônico (GTA), formado por 355 organizações não-governamentais (ONGs) do Brasil, apresentará hoje, em Los Angeles, uma série de propostas que pedem a proibição do desmatamento pelos proprietários com mais de 100 hectares e uma reforma agrária ecológica. O GTA deve sugerir uma campanha para pressionar o Brasil a ampliar as reservas extrativistas. **Pág. A9**

Capitão de 70 exige Zagallo fora da Copa

O capitão do time campeão mundial de 1970, Carlos Alberto Torres, afirma que a única saída da seleção brasileira para tentar evitar um fracasso na Copa da França, será a troca do técnico. "Zagallo é superado", diz Carlos Alberto, comandando por esses tempos na conquista do tricampeonato e agora incomformado com o mau futebol exibido pela seleção na Copa Ouro. Os ex-jogadores Tostão e Júnior são contra o afastamento de Zagallo, mas aprovam a decisão da CBF, antecipada pelo Estado, de contratar um auxiliar. Zagallo chegou ao Rio e diz não ser contrário à indicação de um assessor. **Pág. E1**
O Palmeiras derrotou o São Paulo por 2 a 1 e o Santos empatou com o Botafogo, sem gol, ontem à noite, pelas semifinais do Rio-São Paulo. **Págs. E1 e E3**

Autocrítica
Romário chega ao Rio e reconhece que falhou na Copa Ouro, nos Estados Unidos; mas já está na lista de Zagallo para a França, o atacante evita prosseguir a polêmica com Pelé. **Pág. E1**

Agressão em Nagano
A canadense Geraldine Heaney chuta a jogadora americana Tara Mounsey, na final de hóquei, vencida pelos EUA. **Pág. E4**

Verbas de R$ 181 mi empurraram votação **Pág. A6**
Mangueira dá aula de samba a japoneses **Pág. C1**
Estudo revela que alunos de Oxford escrevem mal **Pág. A12**
Judith Pfaff representa os EUA na Bienal **Pág. D1**
Polícia investiga morte de executiva em SP **Pág. C1**
Carros de placas 5 e 6 estão no rodízio hoje **Pág. C1**

Coleção Castelo Rá-Tim-Bum Estadão
No dia 22/2 não haverá circulação da Coleção Castelo Rá-Tim-Bum, mas estaremos de volta no dia 1/3.

housing, illiteracy, violence, impunity, urban degradation, misuse of natural resources, attacks on the biosphere, shadow politics. When the rainbow appears, our unconscious fantasy might go back to the Covenant, to the reunion and harmony between heavens and earth, an image that might by itself arouse the feeling of hope, compassion, forgiveness, relief from pain, evoking some transcendental force that might one day kindle our hearts and reshape our social shadow.

The Animal World

One front page managed to put together terrorism, violence, and an elephant's tooth. A common first reaction to such an incongruous assemblage is surprise, laughter, amusement. A veterinarian in the local zoo extracted an oversized tooth to alleviate the elephant's pain. So what? That tooth does not fit with national politics, and yet it has intruded into our attention, only to awaken distant information we all have, but do not use, about what is happening on this planet not only with elephants, but with wildlife in general. The tooth was extracted, and now, due to the very incongruity of the image, it lies in our hands.

An intriguing picture taken in northeastern Brazil accompanied a story about a drought. Poor people in that part of the country chronically have to cope with extremely difficult living conditions because of long dry seasons, a century-old problem that goes unsolved because economic resources are never properly allocated in building dams, providing irrigation, or promoting social welfare. Instead, public funds are retained by corrupt officials and local tycoons. Everybody in the country knows it, but the situation stays the same. The image shows no famine, no migrants, no dry landscape—which we all have in our memory. Like many other images that we have seen here, it has a dreamlike, or movie-like quality. In the picture, geese pass in front of a fast-food shop named "Green Sea," but actually this place is far from the tropical shores. There is no green water here, and it has not rained for years. It is now known that geese possess a sharp instinct that orients them toward water, even if it is miles away (elephants have this too, by the way). Humans, unfortunately, lack this capacity, so when a long drought affects a whole region, people wander about with no precise sense of orientation, except the collective notion that they should migrate to larger cities in southern Brazil. São Paulo has for decades hosted such massive currents of social refugees, which results in a displacement of the problem from the rural to the urban milieu. This image, by focusing on the geese, might suggest that instinct, rather than a socially and ideologically conditioned sense of orientation, might have an unexpected part to play in this drama.

Images of the animal world are important for our imagination and thinking, because, as we know—or refuse to know—they might vanish sooner than we expect. If and when that nameless deed happens, it will have been the result of our actions and decisions. We are so dangerously close to this possibility, and we still know so little about them. We still do not understand them and do not appreciate them for what they are, despite their utility, economic value, or the functions they fulfill for us. We still have not developed the capacity to value natural life, in all its forms, for itself, and that is the bottom of the question.

A certain front page illustrated an undisguised archetype of motherhood, a baby gorilla looking at its mother. We could probably still learn something about this relationship by observing animal behavior, as some researchers have been doing, better than by developing projective theories about mother-infant bond. Such theories tell more about our complexes than the workings of the mother archetype. All the attributes of the good mother are present in this female gorilla; yet, in my country, this animal is seen as a clown or a brute, and its name is used in a pejorative way. Immediately below the gorillas' picture, the newspaper printed a picture of an athlete being treated for some neurological malfunction. The newspaper makes us perceive, willingly or not, the archetype of caring and nurturing and the evident similarity between us and them.

On the same page, a helicopter performs an emergency landing in a highway, "while," we might say, a human hand touches a baby anteater (see figure 7). We have no contact whatsoever with anteaters. For most of us, they could be extra-terrestrials. We simply kill them. We do not know who they are, how they behave, about their unique way of being. An image such as this might make us briefly wonder why we do not relate to animals on a deeper level.

O ESTADO DE S. PAULO

Julio Mesquita (1891-1927) — Julio de Mesquita Filho (1927-1969) — Francisco Mesquita (1927-1969) — Julio de Mesquita Neto (1969-1996)

ANO 119 — TERÇA-FEIRA — Nº 38.121
SÃO PAULO, 3 DE MARÇO DE 1998

RUY MESQUITA
Diretor-responsável

ACM pede a cassação de Sérgio Naya

Entrada de dólares no País bate recorde

O ingresso líquido de US$ 6,28 bilhões no País em fevereiro, recorde histórico no mercado de taxas livres, não é motivo de comemoração para o governo, que continua pregando cautela. Mesmo que a entrada de recursos tenha recomposto as reservas internacionais perdidas com a crise asiática, a ordem no BC tem sido a de "não baixar a guarda". A balança comercial registrou déficit de US$ 214 milhões em fevereiro, o menor desde maio de 97, quando o saldo negativo foi de US$ 101 milhões. **Pág. B1**

Unifesp critica gratificação a professores

O Conselho de Graduação da Universidade Federal de São Paulo (Unifesp) é contra o programa de gratificações para docentes com doutorado e mestrado, anunciado pelo governo. O conselho alega que as gratificações não são requisitos salariais. Hoje, uma assembléia define a posição da categoria. A mobilização dos professores faz parte da avaliação nacional que está ocorrendo nas instituições de ensino superior. No fim de semana, um encontro nacional, em Brasília, discutirá uma eventual greve de protesto contra a reforma no ensino. **Pág. A6**

CBF confirma coordenador para a seleção

A Confederação Brasileira de Futebol (CBF) confirmou ontem que Zagallo terá um coordenador técnico na seleção que disputará a Copa do Mundo. O nome do coordenador será anunciado amanhã. Depois de duas reuniões com o treinador, o presidente da entidade, Ricardo Teixeira, disse que gostaria de repetir a fórmula que deu certo em 94. **"Pela responsabilidade do Congresso", na pág. A3**
Pág. E1

Presidente do Senado também defende o fim da imunidade parlamentar no caso de crime comum

O presidente do Senado, Antônio Carlos Magalhães (PFL-BA), pediu ontem à Câmara uma ação "rápida e vigorosa" para cassar o mandato do deputado Sérgio Naya (PPB-MG). Ao Poder Judiciário, solicitou a determinação imediata do seqüestro e da entrega dos bens do parlamentar aos moradores do Edifício Palace 2, que desabou no domingo de carnaval e foi implodido sábado no Rio. Segundo ACM, a demora na cassação "não fará bem nem ao Judiciário nem ao Legisla*tivo"*. Já o seqüestro dos bens, disse, "é indispensável" para garantir a indenização das vítimas". O senador afirmou que, se for consultado pelo PFL, vai propor ao partido que feche questão pela cassação de Naya. Além disso, anunciou que se encarregará da outra iniciativa que o caso mostrou ser indispensável: a revisão das normas da Carta que asseguram imunidade parlamentar frente ao caso de crimes comuns. Porta-voz do Planalto, Sérgio Amaral, disse que a opinião do presidente Fernando Henrique Cardoso sobre a imunidade coincide com a do senador. **Pág. C1**

Resgate
Helicóptero da Polícia Militar sobrevoa a Avenida 23 de Maio para auxiliar no socorro a um motorista acidentado que ficou preso nas ferragens de uma Kombi, no Viaduto Tutóia; bombeiros impediram que o veículo despencasse na pista congestionada **Pág. C7**

Já há 4 mil desabrigados no Ribeira

A cheia do Rio Ribeira do Iguape, que desde o fim de semana castiga o Vale do Ribeira, no sul do Estado de São Paulo, deve atingir hoje com maior intensidade a cidade de Registro. A Defesa Civil estima em mais de 4 mil o número de desabrigados nos municípios da região. A cidade de Iguape deve ver a mais atingida amanhã. As prefeituras de Iporanga, Eldorado, Jacupiranga, Sete Barras e Registro decretaram estado de calamidade. A zona rural foi a mais prejudicada. As plantações de banana, base da economia da região, ficaram submersas. Segundo o diretor do Departamento de Águas e Energia Elétrica (Daee) da região, Ney Ikeda, a preocupação atual é com a remoção das mais que moram em áreas de risco. "O pessoal só decide sair quando não dá mais tempo." **Pág. C3**

Justiça condena Maluf e Pitta por precatórios

A Justiça de São Paulo condenou ontem, em primeira instância, o ex-prefeito Paulo Maluf e o atual prefeito, Celso Pitta, ambos do PPB, em processo no qual são acusados de desvio de R$ 1,23 bilhão no caso dos precatórios. O juiz Venício de Paula Salles, da 9.ª Vara da Fazenda Pública, determinou a suspensão dos direitos políticos por quatro anos dos dois acusados. Contra Pitta foi aplicada a pena acessória de perda do cargo. Ele e Maluf poderão recorrer da condenação. Segundo a sentença, Maluf e Pitta também terão de pagar multa equivalente a 80 vezes o valor da ressurreição que receberam na época da aplicação indevida do dinheiro dos precatórios. Pitta ocupava o cargo de secretário municipal de Finanças. O ex-operador da Dívida Pública da Prefeitura Wagner Ramos também foi condenado. **Pág. A4**

Renúncia é saída para o deputado

RICARDO AMARAL

Amigos do deputado Sérgio Naya, dono do Serven-Eng, acham que ele precisa de um caixa de US$ 10 milhões para cuidar de sua defesa. Embora possua patrimônio calculado em US$ 300 milhões, teria sérias dificuldades para reunir essa quantia. Seu patrimônio é alto, mas de baixa liquidez. Naya ainda confia no corporativismo da Câmara para escapar da cassação, mas admite a hipótese de renunciar ao mandato para recuperar em outubro. **Pág. C1**

Estalos no Palace 1 assustam a Barra

Moradores das proximidades do condomínio de prédios com entradas em Jóquei novamente te, por causa dos estalos na madrugada e na tarde de ontem no Edifício Palace 1, que está interditado. O prédio é vizinho do Palace 2, implodido depois de ter desabado parcialmente e causado a morte de oito pessoas. Os estalos despertaram preocupação, mas não interromperam o trabalho de remoção dos escombros do Palace 2. Os bombeiros ainda não localizaram o corpo do engenheiro Gerardo Queiroz. **Pág. C2**

Vale sob as águas
O trabalhador Deli Rodrigues dos Santos atravessa um trecho alagado da estrada que liga Sete Barras a Eldorado; a maior dificuldade da Defesa Civil é remover moradores das áreas de risco

Pressa no novo Código Penal irrita juristas **Pág. A6**

ONU não aprova ataque automático ao Iraque **Pág. A12**

Microsoft recua e abre espaço para concorrentes **Pág. B7**

Poupança teve perda de R$ 3 bi em fevereiro **Pág. B3**

Terapias em spas ajudam a combater o estresse

Carros de finais 3 e 4 estão no rodízio hoje

Vida de tamanduá
Filhote de tamanduá-de-colete, de 800 g, brinca no Zôo de São Paulo, depois de ser alimentado; ele recebia uma mistura à base de creme de leite, mel e ovo que imitava o leite materno **Pág. A8**

A man who rescued a dog from drowning in a flood got so attached to it that neither one could leave the other. A picture of the pair invokes a positive, mind-inspiring image of a bond between humans and animals. The feeling is also present in a scene of a man rescuing a frightened horse from imminent death.

A newspaper photograph featured two birds of different species: a tiny common city bird feeding an abandoned nestling. This bird, often alluded to as a metaphor, is known, as an adult, for its habit of eating other birds' eggs in the nest. Do we not have here an image of animal compassion, tolerance, and positive inter-racial relationship that hits the core of human alienation and selfishness?

I encountered an image of a unique bird, a truly archetypal architect, that builds nests—actually houses—out of mud. These little huts are cleverly built and located. A bending at the entrance prevents snakes or other predators from entering them to steal eggs or chicks. The birds are stable and monogamous, and they can be regarded as a remote attempt by nature to experiment with the archetype of a nuclear family living in a single house, long before humans developed that form. Building joint nests is an innovation. Greater São Paulo has eighteen million inhabitants, and there is practically no space left for new housing. So the birds express the situation and adapt to the housing shortage problem by building skyscrapers, or new urban development experiments of cohabitation. People living in the neighborhood told the reporter that some of these houses are "for rent," having been used by the first owners and then abandoned. Young couples would then make second-hand use of these available homes, instead of taking the trouble to build new ones—as is the pattern of behavior in the countryside. This image brings to mind the insight that birds and humans are in the same boat.

On another mind-intriguing front page, scientists are researching a particular phosphoric substance in lightning bugs (see figure 8). The idea is that the chemical element that creates that typical green light might be an innovative cancer treatment. Here we are between science and poetry. In alchemy, where such ideas were common, the green light was the healing light of nature, *lumen naturae,* a new understanding of reality hidden in the unconscious.[2] In this same line of imaginal

O ESTADO DE S. PAULO

SÁBADO, 25 DE ABRIL DE 1998 — ANO 119 — N° 38.174

Shoppings apostam no Dia das Mães

Lojistas investiram R$ 3,4 milhões em promoções com o objetivo de superar o resultado das vendas do ano passado; eles oferecem prêmios como automóveis e viagens aos consumidores

Os principais shoppings de São Paulo ampliaram o período de promoções e investiram R$ 3,4 milhões (25% a mais do que em 1997) na tentativa de superar os resultados do Dia das Mães do ano passado. Muitos shoppings esperam um crescimento de até 25% nas vendas do período, mas é "mercado está difícil e não dá para ficar metas ambiciosas", segundo Nabil Sahyoun, presidente da Abshop, que representa 230 estabelecimentos no Estado. Levantamento da Abshop mostra que o otimismo se deve à abertura do comércio aos domingos, que tem impulsionado as vendas. De acordo com Sahyoun, porém, a inadimplência e o desemprego já afetaram os negócios no primeiro trimestre, o que levou os shoppings a investir mais em promoções. Havia expectativa de aumento de 10% nas vendas de janeiro a março, mas verificou-se redução de 6%. Para reverter a tendência nos próximos 15 dias, o Iguatemi está investindo 65% a mais na campanha do Dia das Mães e o Eldorado, quase 50%. A maioria dos shoppings optou pelo sorteio de um carro (o mínimo para participar é de R$ 70), mas também são oferecidos outros prêmios, como uma viagem para qualquer parte do mundo, de acordo com o sonho do consumidor que tenha gasto pelo menos R$ 30. **Pág. B1**

Luz da ciência — Cientistas utilizaram o estudo da capacidade dos vaga-lumes de transformar energia química em luminosa (detalhe) e conseguiram desenvolver novo método de diagnóstico; laboratórios usam o procedimento para detectar vírus como o do HIV **Pág. A16**

Seca deixa 10 milhões em "situação crítica" no NE

Cerca de 10 milhões de pessoas já vivem em "situação crítica" por causa da seca que atinge 1.209 dos 1.787 municípios do Nordeste, principalmente nos Estados de Pernambuco, Alagoas, Ceará e Paraíba, segundo a Sudene. A distribuição de cestas básicas na região começa na próxima semana. A maior seca dos últimos anos deverá reduzir a produção total da safra brasileira de 1997/98, calculada em 80,8 milhões de toneladas de grãos e fibras. A perda em alguns Estados está variando em até 70%. **Págs. A14 e B3**

Homem que matou analista espera júri por outro crime

A polícia prendeu ontem Carlos Eduardo Custódio da Silva, de 22 anos, que confessou ter assassinado o analista Luiz Eduardo Ferraz de Camargo, de 42, funcionário do Cetesb. A PM chegou ao criminoso por meio de uma denúncia anônima. Camargo foi morto na frente das duas filhas, tentando defendê-las de dois assaltantes que invadiram sua casa, na zona sul, na noite de quarta-feira. Silva já cumpria pena de 3 anos de prisão, por assalto, e aguardava em liberdade o julgamento por outro assassinato. **Pág. C1**

Justiça e seqüestradores de Diniz podem fechar acordo

Os seqüestradores do empresário Abílio Diniz podem suspender a greve de fome, que hoje completa 13 dias, na Penitenciária do Estado. O juiz-corregedor da Vara das Execuções Criminais, Octavio Machado de Barros Filho, confirmou ontem o avanço das negociações por um acordo: se os presos suspenderem o protesto, a Justiça estudará a possibilidade de rever os processos. Em outra etapa, os seqüestradores poderão ficar em regime semi-aberto, trabalhando fora durante o dia e pernoitando na prisão. **Pág. C10**

FORTUNE

As 100 maiores forças dos EUA

O suplemento traz a relação das cem maiores empresas americanas. A General Motors lidera o ranking, com US$ 170 bilhões, e a Xerox, em lucro, com US$ 8,46 bilhões.

NOTAS E INFORMAÇÕES

É chegada a hora em que não se pode mais ter os olhos postos nas reivindicações menores dos eleitores, mas sim no favor do Estado brasileiro. As reformas devem vir com urgência, em benefício de todo o País. "Não há tempo a perder", no **pág. A3**

TEMPO

SUAS CONTAS

HOJE 146 páginas

Paula volta à seleção com entusiasmo

Paula integrou-se ontem à seleção brasileira, em São Paulo, e faz hoje o primeiro treino no Rio, preparando-se para o Campeonato Mundial Feminino de Basquete. O Brasil estreia na competição em 26 de maio, contra a Coréia do Sul, em Münster (Alemanha). Aos 36 anos, Paula explicou que volta ao time com entusiasmo. "Sempre tive amor pela seleção", disse, emocionada. A jogadora mostrou tristeza ao falar do pai, Eberard da Silva, que morreu recentemente, mas animou-se em seguida: "Ele gostaria de me ver de novo na seleção". **Pág. E7**

Emoção — Paula enxuga uma lágrima ao falar da morte do pai

Paulistão terá finalista hoje no Morumbi

O primeiro finalista do Campeonato Paulista sai hoje, no Morumbi, no clássico São Paulo x Palmeiras. Às TVs Globo, Record e Bandeirantes mostram o jogo, às 16 horas. O São Paulo, com a melhor campanha da fase anterior, bateu o Palmeiras por 2 a 1, domingo, pelas semifinais, e leva a vantagem de poder até perder por um gol de diferença. O time palmeirense terá Arce, apenas multado em R$ 1.500,00 pelo TJD, e precisa vencer por dois gols. O outro finalista do Paulistão será conhecido amanhã, no jogo Corinthians x Portuguesa. **Pág. E1**

IMPOSTO DE RENDA
Últimas dicas para entregar a declaração **Pág. B8**

Empresa investirá na importação de gás
Direto da Fonte, pág. B2

Suspensa assembléia sobre divisão da Telebrás **Pág. B9**

ACM vai reforçar a mobilização por reformas **Pág. A4**

Bispos criticam lentidão do governo na área social **Pág. A13**

Vicentinho diz que CUT pode dar apoio a saques **Pág. B4**

INSS do Rio começa a exonerar funcionários **Pág. A5**

Kit Legal Estadão
Não perca, amanhã.

Coberturas duplex no Quintas.
Você vai chegar ao topo.

O ESTADO DE S. PAULO

Julio Mesquita (1891-1927) — *Julio de Mesquita Filho (1927-1969)* — ANO 119 QUINTA-FEIRA N° 38.109 SÃO PAULO, 19 DE FEVEREIRO DE 1998 — *Francisco Mesquita (1927-1969)* — *Julio de Mesquita Neto (1949-1996)*

RUY MESQUITA
Diretor-responsável

Para BID, efeito Ásia na América Latina já passou

Estudo conclui que o pior momento da crise está superado nos países latino-americanos, mas o sub-secretário do Tesouro dos EUA adverte que os problemas asiáticos não desapareceram

O Banco Interamericano de Desenvolvimento (BID) conclui que a América Latina superou o pior da crise asiática, mas a região atravessará um período de desaceleração econômica por causa daquela dos preços de commodities como cobre e petróleo. Em relatório com suas previsões para 1998, o BID calcula que o crescimento d'a América Latina, este ano, chegará a 3%, em relação aos 5,2% de 1997. O Brasil está entre os países que crescerão menos, com previsão de expansão do Produto Interno Bruto abaixo de 1%, segundo o economista-chefe do BID, o uruguaio Ricardo Hausmann. O México deverá ter desempenho similar melhor, com crescimento de 3%. O sub-secretário do Tesouro dos EUA, Lawrence Summers, adverte, porém, que a crise asiática ainda não terminou e vai prosseguir causando instabilidade sobre a subavaliação. Nessa avaliação, informa o correspondente em Washington, **Paulo Sotero**, o subsecretário observa que há um consenso entre os países de que a fórmula para enfrentar a crise e evitar que ela se repita em outras áreas passa pela promoção da política de livre mercado. **Págs. B14 e B5**

A busca do antídoto
Taturana-assassina passa por processo de depilação com pinça e tesoura, em laboratório do Instituto Butantã; os pêlos de 4 mil delas estão sendo utilizados na produção de antídoto contra o seu veneno, que pode ser mortal   **Pág. A10**

Chuvas ameaçam viagens no carnaval

O paulistano que deixar a cidade para passar o carnaval no litoral ou no interior pode enfrentar problemas nas estradas. Se a chuva continuar, haverá risco de queda de barreiras e novos pontos na pista. A Operação Descida começa hoje às 9 horas. A partir de amanhã, será adotado o esquema 5x2 – descida por três faixas da Imigrantes e duas da Anchieta. Os bancos e as repartições públicas estaduais e municipais de São Paulo fecham amanhã e voltam a funcionar quarta-feira. **Pág. C1**

Papa acelera promoções no clero

O papa João Paulo II acenou à nomeação de três bispos para o Brasil. A decisão eleva para 13 o total de promoções feitas no prazo de 60 dias, considerada curto para a Igreja. As nomeações e a criação de três circunscrições são vistas como resposta do papa ao clero brasileiro, que reclama da lentidão da Santa Sé. Os padres promovidos pelo papa são Jacinto Furtado, que assumirá como bispo de Cratéus (CE); Geraldo Dantas de Andrade, futuro bispo-auxiliar de São Luís (MA), e Sérgio Arthur Braschi, indicado para auxiliar em Curitiba. **Pág. A12**

Preso membro de gangue que ataca prédios

A polícia prendeu ontem um dos quatro ladrões que aterrorizaram moradores de apartamentos de Pinheiros e Moema na noite de terça-feira. Fernando Canazza, de 20 anos, confessou a participação em assaltos a disse que foi fácil entrar em algumas prédios, pelas garagens. Desempregado, ele unia-se a três outros homens para roubar automóveis importados, jóias e dinheiro. Usando revólveres, a gangue ameaçava algumas vítimas e chegou a trocar tiros com a polícia. **Pág. C7**

NOTAS E INFORMAÇÕES
Vencer a crise na Ásia é o item mais urgente da pauta econômica internacional. A grande meta passa a ser a criação de mecanismos para prever e evitar novas turbulências de grandes proporções. "Segurança para a expansão mundial", **na pág. A3**

Fim do mistério
O finlandês Mika Hakkinen testa a McLaren-Mercedes, no Circuito da Catalunha, em Barcelona; o carro ganhou novo motor, novo sistema de freios e será um dos mais velozes da Fórmula 1, no início da temporada, que começa dia 8, na Austrália. **Pág. 13**

Secretário da ONU tentará saída pacífica

O secretário-geral da ONU, Kofi Annan, acredita que tem "uma chance razoável" de evitar um ataque liderado pelos EUA contra o Iraque e disse ontem que recebeu "total apoio" do Conselho de Segurança para a missão de paz que fará no fim de semana em Bagdá. O governo norte-americano demonstrou pessimismo. **Pág. A15**

Comissão do PT absolve amigo de Lula

O advogado Roberto Teixeira, compadre de Luiz Inácio Lula da Silva, foi absolvido pela Comissão de Ética do PT da acusação, feita pelo petista Paulo de Tarso Venceslau, de ter se aproveitado da amizade de Lula para lhe ficiar sua empresa, CPEM. Ela prometia a prefeituras elevar a arrecadação de ICMS. **Pág. A13**

KATIA ZERO
A nova cara do comércio

NOVA YORK – Ao criar a megaboutique de luxo, os designers conseguiram o impossível: vender exclusividade (butique) às massas (mega). Belo palavrão! Ou seja, implodiram o conceito "butique", que era exclusividade para poucos. É um viva à globalização e o mundo cada vez mais ao alcance de qualquer um. Não tem dinheiro para um terno de US$ 4 mil de Calvin Klein? Saia com a xícara de US$ 30.   **Página D1**

Piso da entrada da Versace, na Quinta Avenida, cujo aluguel é de US$ 50 milhões por ano; a loja vende de móveis a roupas de cama e lingerie

Collor consegue reduzir multa da Receita Federal **Pág. A6**

Apontado gene que pode ser o da reversão sexual? **Pág. A13**

Camdessus faz exigência à Rússia por empréstimo **Pág. A17**

Edmundo rejeita reserva e volta para o Brasil **Pág. 12**

São Paulo registra deflação de 0,04% **Pág. B1**

Chapas com finais 7 e 8 estão no rodízio hoje

COLEÇÃO SUPERTÍTULOS
AMANHÃ, 20/2, SEM PERDÃO.
FREDERICK FORSYTH
São paulino

COMPRE O ESTADÃO E COM MAIS R$ 3,50 LEVE O BEST SELLER.

TEMPO
SUAS CONTAS

HOJE 120 páginas
Classificados 10.516 ofertas

CIUDAD DEL ESTE

FIGURE 9

research we could place this picture of a dangerous caterpillar (see figure 9), whose poison is so lethal and concentrated that it can kill a man instantaneously. Nature: curing or killing. These two images can trigger in the viewer, consciously or not, the homeopathic principle that like cures like and of working with disparate polarities.

Related to the habitat of the animal world, a dramatic picture of huge tree trunks being transported for sale triggers our consciousness about the consequences of the progressive destruction of the largest rain forest in the world. Sometimes the media come up with metaphors that make the situation more promptly understandable, such as saying that so many soccer fields together are being destroyed every minute. Our daily consciousness is reluctant to take in information of this type, which might put us, over breakfast, in bitter contact with the most urgent problems of humanity, its destructive actions, its harmful unconsciousness, and the imminent danger that hovers over the plant and animal world.

I found a story on the aftermath of an oil spill illustrated by what looked like a bronze statuette. It is actually a desperate water bird, immobilized by dark, thick oil penetrating its feathers. We are growing callously accustomed to ecological disasters, this time in Rio. In the picture, the bird spreads its wings open to dry in the warm sun, but to no avail. The image seemingly conveys the hopeless creature's plea for mercy.

In my first dream after I began analysis in Zurich in 1978, I saw two fishes in a pond. Heinrich Karl Fierz, a close disciple and collaborator of Jung, asked me if I had ever heard that the old alchemists wrote about two fishes swimming in opposite directions. He then opened a book and showed me a picture from a seventeenth-century work called "The Lambspring Figures."[3] People begin analysis hoping that the opposites will constellate, and consciousness will start to develop a new relationship with some unconscious content—in my case, the fish. More than twenty years later, I found this very same image—two fishes agonizing in a polluted pond—on a prosaic newspaper page. The fish represent a collective problem of the Piscean era, the splitting or coming together of the opposites. Even a disposable piece of paper can be a mirror for the soul.

The Dream World

The image of a bridge that seems to lead to infinity, as the paper shows, sometimes visits us in our dreams or in idle imagination. The language of dreams wants to be understood by consciousness and culture. Our task is to realize that desire. People who undergo analysis—and poets—develop a way of speaking through images that is clearly richer than the prevalent language of abstractions. Contact with dreams and imagination teaches us a particular way of describing inner reality and to follow the strange logic of images in transformation. This is definitely a development, a cultural step forward: we become sensitive to dreams both inside and outside, and we detect the subtle mirror relationship they have with us. This is a source of knowledge and inspiration that transcends language. Meaning starts to glow in minute events and experiences of everyday life.

The paper sometimes shows pictures of flooded areas of the town. Most people, at least once, have had a dream in which part of their house is covered by water—the garden, the backyard, the lounge, the bathroom. Water is all around their bed, inside their drawers. Water invades their habitat. An unconscious part of the psyche presents itself forcefully to be acknowledged as such, imposingly, irresistibly. Or then, garbage appears in all sorts of inadequate places. Garbage can be a very dirty shadow, or, as *prima materia*, the place in which the emerald was lost. It can be many things and also a complex urban problem. In the paper, garbage and birds (see figure 10) take us directly to psychic complexities.

Every week or so, in my daily practice, I hear airplane dreams. They take off, fall down, do loops, explode, land in weird places or do not land at all, go nowhere. Passengers forget luggage or lose their passports. Their route to the airport is blocked. They miss their plane; their father pilots it. Images of aircraft crashes represent at the same time a common dreadful inner image, the fear that coming down is disastrous—perhaps because above and below, ideology and reality, are so split apart.

The next front page image is what was modern in a town one hundred years ago (see figure 11). Dream images play freely with time,

O ESTADO DE S. PAULO

EDIÇÃO FINAL

Julio Mesquita (1891-1927) — *Julio de Mesquita Filho (1927-1969)* — ANO 118 — DOMINGO — N° 38.035 — *Francisco Mesquita (1927-1969)* — *Julio de Mesquita Neto (1969-1996)*

SÃO PAULO, 7 DE DEZEMBRO DE 1997

RUY MESQUITA
Diretor-responsável

Governadores já trabalham pela reeleição

Levantamento do *Estado* mostra que só dois já decidiram não se candidatar; ritmo de obras, da propaganda na TV e da contratação de publicitários revela que a campanha começou

SILVIO BRESSAN
e RICARDO OSMAN

Pelo menos 20 governadores já decidiram candidatar-se à reeleição e outros 5 tendem a seguir o mesmo caminho, segundo levantamento feito pelo Estado. Apenas dois — Vítor Buaiz (PT), do Espírito Santo, e Wilson Martins (PMDB), do Mato Grosso do Sul — mostram-se decididos a deixar o posto no ano que vem. Com a inédita possibilidade da reeleição, a maioria dos governadores vai entrar em 98 com o pé no palanque, inaugurando obras, acabadas ou não. Como sempre, o governante estará trabalhando para um candidato, só que desta vez será ele próprio. Entre os indecisos, Tasso Jereissati (PSDB-CE) só vai para o "sacrifício" da reeleição se surgir alguém capaz de ameaçar os tucanos, há 12 anos no poder no Estado. Por motivos diferentes, Almir Gabriel (PSDB), do Pará, Paulo Souto (PFL), da Bahia, e Manoel Gomes de Barros (PTB), de Alagoas, também vacilam. Fora esses, todos os governadores são candidatos, embora alguns não o confirmem. Mas o frenético ritmo das obras, da propaganda na TV e da contratação de publicitários denuncia a campanha começou. São os casos de Marcello Alencar (PSDB), do Rio, e até do inspetivamente mesmo candidato de hoje, o tucano Mário Covas, de São Paulo. **Páginas A4 e A5**

Briga por espaço
Em estações de tratamento e nos dois aterros usados para receber o lixo da cidade, jamelões disputam território entre detritos

Tratamento do lixo desafia São Paulo

São Paulo, a maior cidade da América Latina, está batendo outro recorde: a produção diária de 12,5 mil toneladas de lixo. Enquanto a população de São Paulo cresceu 3% nos últimos seis anos, o volume de lixo domiciliar produzido na capital aumentou 32%. Faltam locais adequados para receber os detritos domésticos e industriais. Apenas 0,5% do lixo domiciliar é reciclado. A Prefeitura gasta R$ 1,2 milhão por dia com a coleta, destinação e tratamento do lixo. **Páginas C4 e C5**

Sindicatos tentam saída contra o desemprego

Depois de os setores automotivo e eletroeletrônico terem iniciado a discussão sobre redução de jornada e salários, diante da perspectiva de aumento do desemprego, outras áreas da produção mostram disposição de debater mudanças. Houve demissões no vestuário, em fábricas de calçados e no setor químico, além da antecipação de férias coletivas. Sindicatos e empresas prevêem maior desemprego. **Página B1**

Vestibulandos procuram ajuda de psicólogo

Cada vez mais, o desgaste emocional provocado pela tensão e pela proximidade do vestibular tem levado muitos estudantes a procurar o auxílio de psicólogos. As queixas mais freqüentes são distúrbios do sono, mudanças no apetite, crises de choro e briga em família. Cansados da rotina de estudo, esses jovens têm dificuldade em manter a calma quando precisam enfrentar a maratona de exames. Neste domingo, 138.497 candidatos fazem provas de Geografia, História, Biologia e Matemática, na segunda etapa da primeira fase da Fuvest, o mais disputado vestibular do País. Os portões dos locais de exame serão fechados às 13h30, pontualmente. **Página A19**

NOTAS E INFORMAÇÕES
Uma união aduaneira é caracterizada pela existência de uma tarifa externa comum. No caso do Mercosul, essa união torna-se imperfeita diante da vasta lista de exceções à regra das tarifas. *"Amoaça real do Mercosul", na página A3*

TEMPO *(quadro)*
SUAS CONTAS *(quadro)*
HOJE 290 Páginas
Tiragem 628.011

Resultado de Kyoto pode ser frustração

PAULO SOTERO
Kyoto

Às negociações dos cinco dias da conferência de Kyoto levaram a contornos de um livre fracasso do acordo sobre o controle das emissões dos gases responsáveis pelo aquecimento da atmosfera. O agente pode deixar os ambientalistas frustrados e os poluidores aliviados. **Página A12**

Estônia vê a extinção de povo milenar

Aos 80 anos, Pauline Klavina convive com o peso da história: ela é um dos quatro remanescentes dos livonianos, povo que durante 5 mil anos dominou os mares gelados dos países bálticos. Sua cultura e sua língua estão em extinção na Estônia. Metade das 6 mil línguas faladas no mundo tende a desaparecer. **Página A18**

Jovens têm pressa de maioridade

Cerca de 9 milhões de jovens brasileiros entre 18 e 21 anos poderão ter, no ano que vem, direito de abrir empresas e casar, entre outras atividades que, para eles, ainda são proibidas por lei. Mas isso, só depois que o Congresso aprovar mudança no Código Civil que baixa a maioridade dos 21 para os 18 anos. Hoje, o jovem que quiser montar um negócio, como Cláudia Cunha, de 19 anos, tem de passar pelo processo de reconhecimento de firmas, testemunhas e declaração que já esteja registrada em cartório. Também por ser "incapaz", o estudante Fabricio dos Reis, de 20 anos, está se emancipando para poder receber do pai um apartamento de presente. Cláudia reclama por causa do tempo que perdeu e dos R$ 100 que teve de gastar. Mesmo assim, cresce o número de emancipações no 1º Registro Civil de São Paulo, órgão da Praça da Sé. Este ano a média mensal é de 538 registros, enquanto no ano passado foi de 473. **Página A17 e A18**

Tragédia no frio
Avião cai na Sibéria e causa dezenas de mortes **Página A22**

VIDEOMAGIA
Filme deste domingo mostra aventura na selva amazônica **Página A33**

CD-JT
Está nas bancas o rock rural de Sá & Guarabyra **Página A22**

CLASSIFICADOS	172 páginas
IMOVEIS	34 páginas
AUTOS	36 páginas
EMPREGOS	
OPORTUNIDADES	22 páginas

Caderno 2
2 páginas
Suplemento Feminino
Casa & Família
Telejornal
8 páginas

COLEÇÃO SUPERTÍTULOS
NA PRÓXIMA 6ª NO ESTADÃO

DIA 12/12 - AGATHA CHRISTIE
(ASSASSINATO NO CAMPO DE GOLFE)
COMPRE O ESTADÃO E COM MAIS
R$ 3,50 LEVE O BEST SELLER.

Natal deve aumentar venda de supérfluos **Página B3**
Passageiro da ponte aérea optaria por trem **Página A21**
Pitta vai cobrar por conserto de calçadas **Página C7**
Palmeiras termina fase semifinal com vitória **Página E2**
Seleção joga às 15 horas com TV **Página E1**
Tecido leve inova modelos de saias **Feminino**

FIGURE 10

whereas consciousness operates in a rigid space-time continuum. Dreams can picture you today in your nursery, in the Middle Ages or in a situation that has not yet happened, but will, as if we carried inside a dimension in which here and there, past and future, are but one reality. It does good to the soul to look at the newspaper in a rainy morning and see my hometown as it was a century ago, when my grandparents migrated from Italy, and I can only imagine how they felt walking along that street. Or see myself today, in that same street, together, then and now, passionately trying to understand what happened to its soul, and to mine.

One newspaper image depicted a hole that suddenly appeared in the middle of a road. The irritating asphalt deficiency was a door to Hades. As is implosion (see figure 12), getting rid of too much concrete, too much concretism and literalism out there and inside here, those pretentious theoretical edifices of arrogance that keep new spirit away.

Newspapers print sport pictures everyday, and they are often similar. Sometimes, though, we can see in them things they do not intend to reveal. In a bunch of piled up men we catch tribal behavior, a closeness of bodies allowed in the game but forbidden anywhere else. In a macho society, such close contact can only take place after a score. Captions never allude to this overpowering presence of Eros—a fact that collective masculine consciousness refuses to admit—but it is there in the image. In pictures of fans who have painted their faces with the national colors to propitiate victory at a World Cup final we find Indian *participation mystique,* Indian sorcery, Indian face.

Power

Politicians appear everyday, and they try hard to create pseudo events to gain space in the media. As in sports, it is nearly always the same image. In politics, faces hide, eyes lie. The newspaper tries to counteract it by juxtaposing photographs, thus conveying a subliminal, different message. But the interesting thing is that sometimes the structure of the image, or its symbolism, is what carries the more revealing news. On the same page we have Louis XIV and above our president, who behaves like a monarch, a senator who plays his Richelieu, and lying

FIGURE 11

O ESTADO DE S. PAULO

RUY MESQUITA — Diretor-responsável

Julio Mesquita (1891-1927) — *Julio de Mesquita Filho (1927-1969)* — ANO 119 — SÁBADO — Nº 38.118 — SÃO PAULO, 28 DE FEVEREIRO DE 1998 — *Francisco Mesquita (1927-1969)* — *Julio de Mesquita Neto (1969-1996)*

Novo desabamento
A seqüência mostra o momento em que uma nova estrutura do Edifício Palace II desabou, lançando sobre a rua entulho e uma grande quantidade de água que estava acumulada no alto do prédio

Juiz autoriza implosão de prédio no Rio

Queda de escombros começou de madrugada; interdição de 8 edifícios deixou 6 mil desabrigados

O juiz Jessé Torres Pereira Júnior concedeu liminar à prefeitura do Rio, autorizando a implosão do que restou do Edifício Palace II, na Barra da Tijuca. A operação, que exigirá a retirada de 14 mil moradores de casas e prédios vizinhos, está marcada para as 12 horas. Desabou ontem mais uma parte da estrutura dos 22 andares do edifício. O desmoronamento causou pânico entre os moradores da área. À 1h30 da madrugada, caíram duas lajes do alto do prédio. Às 12h55, foi ao chão uma nova coluna de concreto, levando poeira e água. Oito prédios estão interditados, deixando quase 6 mil desabrigados. O delegado Carlos Alberto Pinto, que investiga o desabamento ocorrido domingo, ordenou a interdição da sede da empresa Sersan, construtora do edifício, depois de ter verificado que os escritórios, em Copacabana, estão abandonados. Ele ainda não conseguiu entregar as intimações para o depoimento de três engenheiros, acusados de prédio preventivo. A polícia espera obter, na Sersan, as plantas de estrutura do Edifício Palace II, que até agora não apareceram. Pedaços recolhidos do prédio serão examinados em laboratório para a avaliação da qualidade do material usado na construção. Foi encontrado ontem o corpo de mais uma das vítimas e sete pessoas ainda estão desaparecidas. A busca de outros corpos ocorrerá após a implosão. Conceição Garcia, de 80 anos, te-mendo domingo, apesar de morar a 270 km do local da Barra da Tijuca: ela reside numa pequena casa, o primeiro imóvel projetado pelo deputado Sérgio Naya (PPB-MG), o da empresa Sersan, em Laranjal (MG). **Pág. C1**

Indústria inicia reação e queda do PIB é menor

Ipea e Fiesp apontam crescimento da atividade no mês passado, em relação a dezembro, contrariando as previsões pessimistas; o valor real das vendas também aumentou

Estimativas do Instituto de Pesquisa Econômica Aplicada (Ipea) indicam um crescimento de 6% da atividade da indústria em janeiro em relação a dezembro. Em comparação com janeiro do ano passado, a elevação foi de 1,5%. Os números contrariam as previsões pessimistas feitas depois do pacote fiscal de novembro, quando foi registrada redução de 3,5%, seguida de 5% em dezembro. Com os sinais de recuperação, as últimas projeções da queda de 2% do PIB no primeiro trimestre, feitas pelo Ipea no fim de dezembro, foram revistas para uma redução de apenas 0,7% em relação ao último trimestre de 1997. Dados da Fiesp também demonstram que as expectativas pessimistas não se confirmaram. Segundo a entidade, o nível de atividade da indústria cresceu 3,8% em janeiro, se comparado a janeiro do ano passado, e o valor real das vendas do 2,5% maior. **Pág. B1**

Horário de verão termina à meia-noite

O horário de verão termina à meia-noite de hoje. Os relógios deverão ser atrasados uma hora nos Estados das Regiões Sul, Sudeste e Centro-Oeste, além da Bahia, do Distrito Federal e do Tocantins. Levantamento parcial do Ministério de Minas e Energia mostra que os 146 dias de vigência do horário de verão trouxeram uma economia média de energia de 0,9% e redução de 3,8% na demanda. Os números equivalem ao consumo de Mato Grosso do Sul no mesmo período. **Pág. A10**

Rainha agora passará a agir no Nordeste

O líder do Movimento Sem-Terra (MST) José Rainha Júnior anunciou que pretende transferir sua área de atuação para o Nordeste. Ele afirmou que a missão no Pontal "está cumprida" e em março vai ao Ceará para manter contato com as bases do movimento na região. Rainha admitiu que a atuação do Incra e do governo estadual na obtenção de terras destinadas à reforma agrária no Pontal vem atendendo as reivindicações do MST. **Pág. A13**

Brasil protesta contra informe sobre drogas

O governo brasileiro vai protestar contra o relatório anual sobre drogas divulgado ontem pela ONU. Com base nos dados de 1996, o documento lamenta que "a lavagem de dinheiro ainda não seja considerada crime" no Brasil e critica o País por adiar a adoção de medidas. Projeto sobre lavagem de dinheiro do tráfico de drogas foi aprovado pelo Congresso no ano passado. A legislação será apresentada em reunião da ONU, em março, na Áustria. **Pág. A6**

NOTAS E INFORMAÇÕES
Quando se considera o deficit nominal da União, Estados e municípios, verifica-se que os dois últimos são responsáveis por 51,8% dele, o governo central, por 40,7% e as estatais, pelo restante. Trata-se de uma responsabilidade compartilhada.
"São todos culpados", ver **pág. A3**

Recado a Edmundo
Zagallo, na chegada ao Rio, após passar férias em Nova York, disse que o atacante da Fiorentina tem de acertar sua situação no clube italiano, se quiser manter a esperança de ir à Copa **Pág. C7**

São Paulo joga hoje a 1.ª final com Botafogo

O São Paulo tenta sair na frente, hoje, na decisão de um título que jamais conquistou, o do Torneio Rio-São Paulo, enfrentando o Botafogo na primeira partida das finais, às 16 horas, no Morumbi, com TV. O outro jogo será quarta-feira, no Maracanã. O técnico Nelsinho quer o time paulista agressivo para acumular vantagem antes de ir para o Rio. O Botafogo terá Bebeto e Túlio no ataque. **Pág. E1**

ESPORTES NA TV
14h00 Futebol: África do Sul e Egito — ESPN Brasil
16h00 Futebol: São Paulo x Botafogo — SBT, Globo e SporTV
16h00 Futebol: Juninho x São José — Bandeirantes

Clonagem holandesa
Holly e Belle são as primeiras bezerras clonadas na Holanda; o governo decidiu proibir novas experiências no país **Pág. A11**

Ações lideraram as aplicações em janeiro **Pág. B4**

Sai a terceira lista de aprovados da Fuvest
Classificados

Linha do fura-fila será entregue pela metade **Pág. C13**

Randas Batista deixa hospital e faz denúncia **Pág. A11**

Pitta vai ao STF para mudar correção da dívida **Pág. A8**

Saiba como é feita a previsão do tempo

Coleção Castelo Rá-Tim-Bum Estadão.

in a coffin the senator's son, the would-be next man in power (see figure 13). A cocaine overdose burst his heart. The archetype of the old king's renewal is what gives depth to the picture and to our perception.

Another front page revealed a Shakespearean scene: our president, the first lady, and the same senator trying to charm her. Behind the scenes, he had been plotting to get the president to submit to his own power plans, eventually betraying him. Should we readers just stay with the informative subtitles (who, what, why, when, where, and how) or watch the hidden theatrical drama and its actors? Power archetypes incarnate in politicians every day, everywhere. We can perceive such archetypes better through images than speech.

An image of an ex-president and his daughter, whom he has been preparing as crown princess, betrays an incestuous bond that even the cleverest journalist would be unable to talk about. Who would dare? Only in a picture can anyone see how sensuous she appears to him, what a nice couple they make. A genuine father's daughter in politics, playing a part in a Greek tragedy.

We have an enormous cake in the shape of Lenin (see figure 14). Little girls, usually used by propaganda to prove how sweet strong men can be, are here waiting to get a part of Lenin's body to eat, as in the cannibalistic ritual described by the German adventurer Hans Staden after he was caught by the Tupinambá Indians in sixteenth-century Brazil.[4] For nine months he waited for his ritual death and his consumption by barbarian people who after all, for no apparent reason, left him alive. Eating Lenin as cake would be the imaginal assimilation and digestion, by the new generation, of all the indescribable horrors the Russians and their neighbors had to endure for the sake of freedom and dignity. The newspaper prints it as a joke, but if you connect to the image, the understanding comes immediately to you through the archetype of cannibalism. Do we not do the same, but for different reasons, with the body of Christ? How can the sad folly of the communist fantasy be transformed if it does not get into the bowels?

A newspaper photograph captured a group of Xavante Indians threatening and subduing the National Indian Foundation's president, a man who ruled over their constitutional rights. The picture was taken

O ESTADO DE S. PAULO

SP, RJ, MG, PR e SC: R$ 1,00
Demais Estados: ver tabela na página A4

EDIÇÃO SÃO PAULO

RUY MESQUITA
Diretor-responsável

Julio Mesquita (1891-1927) — *Julio de Mesquita Filho (1927-1969)* — ANO 119 QUINTA-FEIRA Nº 38.173 SÃO PAULO, 23 DE ABRIL DE 1998 — *Francisco Mesquita (1927-1969)* — *Julio de Mesquita Neto (1969-1996)*

Reforma será homenagem a líderes mortos

Presidente diz que o maior tributo que o Congresso poderia prestar a Sérgio Motta e Luís Eduardo Magalhães seria aprovar rapidamente as mudanças constitucionais pelas quais eles tanto se empenharam

O presidente Fernando Henrique Cardoso disse ontem, em Madri, antes de regressar ao Brasil para o enterro do deputado Luís Eduardo Magalhães, que a rápida aprovação das emendas constitucionais, em tramitação no Congresso, é a única saída para efetivar as reformas no País. Abalado e atribuindo a FHC antecipou sua volta da Espanha para o despedir do líder do governo na Câmara. "Espero que o Congresso agora entenda que a melhor homenagem que pode prestar a Luís Eduardo, a melhor saudade que pode também manifestar ao Sérgio (Motta), é mais votarmos essas medidas pelas quais eles se empenharam tanto", apelou. O presidente classificou de duro o golpe e a morte de ambos: "Eu perdi dois irmãos". O velório e o enterro de Luís Eduardo transformaram-se em atos políticos a que gritavam: "Presidente, faça as reformas, em homenagem a Luís Eduardo." Na entrevista que concedeu no momento do desembarque na Base Aérea de Salvador, o presidente conclamou as oposições a pensar mais no Brasil e menos em si próprias. O corpo de Luís Eduardo foi velado no Salão Negro do Congresso, com a presença de grande número de políticos, ministros, juízes, diplomatas e funcionários do governo. O senador Antônio Carlos Magalhães permaneceu ao lado do caído durante quase toda a madrugada, chorando e acariciando o rosto do filho. Foram cerca de 15 horas e meia de angústia, até o desespero, desde que de recebeu o telefonema de Luís Eduardo, avisando que estava passando mal. O caixão, conduzido por cadetes da Polícia Militar, deixou o Congresso às 10 horas, sob aplausos, e chegou a Salvador, onde era aguardado por uma multidão. Muitas pessoas choravam desconsoladamente. Centenas aglomeraram-se perto do caixão e só saíram depois de chegada a PM. Pelas ruas por onde passou o cortejo, pessoas acenavam com camisetas ou bandeiras. O sepultamento foi realizado à noite no Cemitério Campo Santo. **Págs. A4 e A12**

"O governo terá de ter maturidade para reconstruir suas forças políticas no Congresso"
Deputado *Antônio Kandir (PSDB-SP)*

"Pela primeira vez, na vida, está tudo invertido ao lado de ACM, rezando por ele"
Senador *Pedro Simon (PMDB-RS)*

"Não é justo invertermos os fatos e enterrarmos nossos filhos; é uma injustiça, é uma injustiça"
Senador *Antônio Carlos Magalhães*

"Eu não estou preocupado com a questão política; esta é uma questão humana"
Presidente *Fernando Henrique Cardoso*

Amizade — Fernando Henrique Cardoso passa a mão no rosto de Luís Eduardo Magalhães, no velório, em Salvador, pouco após sua chegada da Espanha, sinal de respeito pelo líder do governo na Câmara; Antônio Carlos, em prantos, permanece ao lado do corpo do filho

Mercado fica apreensivo e bolsas caem

A Bolsa de Valores de São Paulo fechou ontem em queda de 2,7%, apontada por especialistas em mercado financeiro como um reflexo da perda de duas forças políticas do País - o ministro das Comunicações, Sérgio Motta, e o deputado Luís Eduardo Magalhães (PFL-BA). No Rio, as perdas da Bolsa chegaram a 4,26%. Não houve ânimo para os negócios. Empresas estrangeiras evitaram aplicar capitais. A volta do presidente Fernando Henrique Cardoso, antecipando-a fim da visita à Espanha, provocou expectativa sobre a possibilidade de o Planalto acelerar mudanças na cúpula do governo. **Pág. B1**

NOTAS E INFORMAÇÕES

A morte inesperada de Luís Eduardo Magalhães foi o segundo golpe sofrido pelo presidente Fernando Henrique Cardoso em menos de 48 horas. Após a perda de Sérgio Motta, o País fica também sem um de seus políticos mais promissores. *"Os golpes do destino"*, na pág. A3

TEMPO
SUAS CONTAS
HOJE   136 páginas
Classificados   9.915 ofertas

Violência do Palmeiras bate recorde

O Palmeiras vive, sob o comando de Luiz Felipe Scolari, o estigma de um dos times mais violentos de São Paulo, dois anos após a conquista do título paulista com uma equipe caracterizada pelo futebol-arte, na fase de Wanderley Luxemburgo. Entre os semifinalistas do Paulistão, o Palmeiras lidera o ranking da indisciplina, com 12 cartões vermelhos e 76 amarelos em 26 jogos. Essa situação é atribuída por alguns jornalistas de São Paulo, a técnico que chegou a agredir um repórter. O treinador afirma ser "perseguido pela imprensa paulista". **Pág. E1**

Emoção e dor — Luís Eduardo chora, ao lado do avô, a morte do pai, momentos antes do enterro; centenas de pessoas aglomeraram-se perto do caixão e só saíram depois que a Polícia Militar chegou

CADERNO 2

DiCaprio volta a enlouquecer fãs

Hollywood procura há anos conquistar os adolescentes. Já tentou ganhar esse público com Tom Cruise e Brad Pitt, mas nenhum deles se compara ao fenômeno Leonardo DiCaprio, que estreia amanhã no papel do rei Luís XIV em O Homem da Máscara de Ferro, depois de levar as garotas ao delírio em Titanic. Elas nunca se contentam em vê-lo apenas uma vez: a prova é que não tem cinema nem comprar só uma revista em que ele apareça. Mas o ator não dá a menor atenção às suas fãs. **Pág. D1**

Promessa de sucesso — Ator estreia como Luís XIV

Cresce em SP a procura por cardiologistas

A morte prematura do deputado Luís Eduardo Magalhães, vítima de enfarte do miocárdio aos 43 anos, provocou uma onda de insegurança entre profissionais que levam vida agitada e estressante. A reportagem do *Estado* constatou um aumento expressivo de pedidos de consultas com especialistas, principalmente cardiologistas, ontem em São Paulo. Para os médicos, esse tipo de preocupação tem seu lado positivo, pois ajuda a prevenir doenças. Eles ressaltam, no entanto, que o mais importante é estar atento aos fatores de risco, entre eles o sedentarismo, a hipertensão e o tabagismo. **Pág. A13**

Índios invadem fazendas em MS

Índios guaranis-caiovás estão invadindo pequenas fazendas em Paranhos, no sul de Mato Grosso do Sul, junto à fronteira com o Paraguai. Eles reivindicam a posse de 4 mil hectares de terras, reconhecidas como de sua propriedade pela Funai. Os conflitos na região existem desde o fim da Guerra do Paraguai, no século passado. **Pág. A16**

Pitta pode ser chamado duas vezes pela CPI

O prefeito Celso Pitta (PPB) poderá ser a primeira autoridade convocada pela Câmara Municipal de São Paulo para depor na CPI da Educação, instaurada ontem. A liderança do PT e 12 vereadores do grupo rebelde pretendem chamar Pitta para depor duas vezes, uma como ex-secretário de Finanças do ex-prefeito Paulo Maluf e outra como atual prefeito. Os vereadores querem a apuração de supostas irregularidades no repasse de verbas federais devidas à educação em últimos anos. Dos sete integrantes da CPI, quatro estão ligados a Pitta. A primeira reunião será hoje, às 10 horas. **Pág. C1**

Universidade será paga na Inglaterra
Pág. A14

Renault usou cadáveres de crianças para testes
Pág. A14

Empresa retira 2.500 pneus do Tietê em 2 meses
Pág. C12

Bispos vão discutir mudanças no batismo
Pág. A15

Zagallo convoca seleção e deixa Müller de fora

Emprego assalariado perde espaço nos anos 90
Pág. B5

Classificados do Estadão.

855-2001

Ligue e anuncie.

Classificados ESTADÃO

A diferença é que o Estadão funciona.

FIGURE 13

O ESTADO DE S. PAULO

MST já ocupa 299 áreas com 200 mil pessoas

O movimento promoveu, apenas neste ano, 42 invasões e o Paraná é o Estado com maior número de acampamentos, 76; no sul do Pará, estão previstas novas ações no prazo de duas semanas

O Movimento dos Sem-Terra (MST) já promoveu este ano 42 ocupações em dez Estados, incluindo as duas no sul do Pará, no fim de semana. O movimento tem agora 299 acampamentos no País, montados em áreas públicas, cedidas ou não pelo governo, e em fazendas invadidas. Neles vivem 57.301 famílias, o que representa 200 mil pessoas alojadas em barracas, segundo o MST. O maior número de acampamentos está no Sul e o Paraná é o campeão, com 76. Ontem o movimento prosseguia com a estratégia de reagir com invasões à morte de dois líderes do MST, quinta-feira, em Paranapebas, sul do Pará: foram ocupadas as Fazendas Serra Norte e Volta do Rio, em Eldorado dos Carajás. Gladson Barbosa, líder do MST no Pará, informou que estão previstas mais invasões, nas duas semanas. As ocupações marcarão a passagem de dois anos do massacre de 19 sem-terra, em Eldorado dos Carajás. A nova onda de invasões foi deflagrada domingo, quando cerca de 300 pessoas voltaram à Goiás 2. Em Paranapebas, o clima é tenso. Na manhã de ontem, uma manifestação de 300 trabalhadores, na frente do Fórum, levou a juíza Maria Vitória do Carmo a solicitar proteção policial. Maria Vitória afastou-se do caso alegando que estiveram na Fazenda Goiás 2, na quinta-feira. **Págs. A10 e A11**

Retalhando o passado — *Um garçom corta em fatias um bolo com o formato da múmia de Lenin, em Moscou, na encenação de um grupo de artistas de vanguarda, simbolizando o fim da União Soviética e a decadência da herança deixada pelo comunismo na Rússia*

Krause pede união contra crime ambiental

O ministro do Meio Ambiente, Gustavo Krause, disse ontem, no debate sobre a Lei de Crimes Ambientais, promovido pelo Estadão e pelo *Jornal da Tarde*, no auditório do Grupo Estado, que a nova legislação "vai pegar" se tiver respaldo do aparato policial dos governos federal, estadual e municipais, além de apoio do Poder Judiciário e dos meios de comunicação. "Todos têm a responsabilidade de fazer dessa lei um instrumento eficaz", afirmou Krause. O governador Mário Covas participou do debate, elogiou a legislação e disse que a defesa do ambiente é principalmente uma "atitude política". O Exército detectou ontem novas queimadas em Roraima e a ONU começou a discutir com o governo brasileiro a ajuda que dará para o combate ao fogo. **Págs. B13 e A14**

Reserva bate recorde no País e chega a US$ 65 bi

O Brasil alcançou reservas internacionais acima de US$ 65 bilhões, um recorde histórico, superando completamente as perdas sofridas na crise asiática. A chefe do Departamento de Operações das Reservas do Banco Central, Maria de Socorro Carvalho, disse ao Estado que os números atuais refletem uma grande recuperação, em setembro, antes da crise, o País acumulava US$ 61,9 bilhões em reservas e, apenas um mês atrás, o total ficava em US$ 58,7 bilhões. Nos dois últimos meses, houve uma recuperação de US$ 12 bilhões. A entrada de dólares aumentou ainda mais na semana passada, superando as previsões otimistas do próprio BC e do mercado. Na sexta-feira, entraram US$ 2,8 bilhões. "Desse dinheiro, 80% foram em empréstimos e captações", explicou Maria do Socorro. Dois consórcios de exploração da banda B de telefonia celular são responsáveis pela chegada de US$ 2 bilhões. **Pág. B1**

Fogo em Roraima — *Pontos vermelhos, na foto de satélite tratada em computador, mostram incêndios na área ianomâmi*

Obras marcam privatização da Castelo-Raposo

O governador Mário Covas assina ontem, em Sorocaba, o contrato de concessão das Rodovias Castelo Branco, Raposo Tavares e Castelinho, que dá à concessão Viaoeste, integrado por seis construtoras, a partir de hoje, o direito de explorar essas estradas por 20 anos, com investimento de R$ 750 milhões. Entre as obras previstas, está a construção de vias marginais no início da Castello, até Alphaville, e a duplicação de 81 km da Raposo. Pela concessão, o Estado receberá R$ 385 milhões e 3% da receita dos pedágios. **Pág. A4**

Prorrogada a negociação de dívida estadual

O governo decidiu ontem prorrogar o prazo de renegociação das dívidas estaduais, previsto originalmente para terminar hoje. A decisão beneficiará diretamente quatro Estados: Rio de Janeiro, Rio Grande do Sul, Acre e Alagoas, que estão apresentando as maiores dificuldades para fechar sua negociação, o prazo será ampliado por 90 dias. Acre e Rio Grande do Sul terão 15 dias para os entendimentos. Para o governador do Rio, Marcello Alencar, foi uma vitória política. **Pág. B4**

Desemprego atinge 7,42%

O índice de desemprego no Brasil chegou a 7,42% da população economicamente ativa em fevereiro, superior a variação de 7,25% registrada em janeiro. Os números, divulgados ontem pelo IBGE, revelam que no mês passado o desemprego atingiu o maior nível verificado em um mês de fevereiro desde 1984, com 1.281 milhão de pessoas sem emprego. A região metropolitana de São Paulo teve o pior resultado da sua história: o desemprego atingiu 8,78%, superior aos 8,51% de janeiro. **Pág. B9**

NOTAS E INFORMAÇÕES
A acusação de um líder do MST contra o presidente Fernando Henrique Cardoso, por causa de incidentes ocorridos no Pará, apresenta erros fundamentais. Para o movimento, coibir invasão é "medida punitiva". "Responsáveis tantos pelo rastro errado", na pág. A3

Presos no Rio assassinos de diretor de hospital **Pág. C7**

Candidatura de Covas causa divisão no PFL **Pág. A8**

Ladrões assaltam pedágio e roubam R$ 363 mil **Pág. C3**

'Estado' entrega hoje Prêmio Top Imobiliário **Pág. A11**

Escócia é roteiro para quem quer evitar o tédio **Viagem**

Corinthians enfrenta o Cruzeiro no Mineirão **Pág. E1**

A HISTÓRIA DE TODOS NÓS.

O BankBoston, em suas nova iniciativa de quem tem compromisso com a cultura, apresenta:
50 Anos de Brasil. Nossa história recente, contada por quem fez parte dela.
31 de março a 3 de abril — 22h30h TV Cultura.

BankBoston

Marmelada milionária
O ex-campeão mundial dos pesos pesados Mike Tyson pega Stone Cold Steve Austin pelo calção para jogá-lo de volta ao ringue durante campeonato de luta livre disputado domingo em Boston, no qual Stone era o desafiante de Shawn Michaels. Tyson, que está suspenso da união de boxe, depois de ter arrancado a dentadas um pedaço da orelha de Evander Holyfield, fez uma participação especial ao torneio de luta livre de Boston e recebeu US$ 3 milhões para simular alguns golpes e arrancar aplausos da plateia. **Pág. E4**

FIGURE 14

on Indian's Day, April 19, one of the several demagogic tributes the government pays to the community that until 1500 owned the land upon which we stand. Power was brutally taken from them, without the least attempt to give them a share or a minimal participation in the decision-making process, even in matters exclusively of their own concern, such as land property or the right to choose their own destiny. The image of a physical struggle in the foundation's headquarters in Brasilia portrays a shift of power. The underdog Indians acquired a few moments of concrete power, only to lose it again in the following day after a harsh admonition to stop it for their own good.

The Anima

The page depicts an actress who got her cherished Oscar and, below, the discovery of the five-thousand-year-old mummy of an Andean girl (see figure 15). The eternal feminine then and today, endless mystique, vanishing beauty, faces frozen in time. Is that all about Eve? Or is there more, and more, always the same, always as if for the first time?

A concretization of the same ideal can be seen in the icon of a Rolls Royce de Luxe sedan turned into a real woman. This supreme car stands for a highly priced object of masculine desire, and it traditionally displays this feminine figure, a modern equivalent of those old wooden carved torsos in a galleon's prow, a true image of wild adventurers' anima challenging the waves of the ocean in order to find gratification in someone else's land. This is a kind of anima that arouses phallic greed for conquest, for gold, sex, slaves, Eldorado, Calcutta, the Moon, luring men to make money and spend it. In automobile and merchandising imagery, this anima figure seems to be inviting potential consumers to the world of success, credit cards, glamour, orgasm, and power.

Jewels and women have always been associated. In one photograph, a glittering blue diamond is akin to a woman's eye. Men want to give such a charming object to their wives or lovers as a token of their love or financial success, while some women lure their men to provide them with status symbols of this kind. Such images fully immerse us in anima psychology, symbolism, and illusions. Another day, we see Evita Perón's

O ESTADO DE S. PAULO

SP, RJ, MG, PR e SC: R$ 1,00
Demais Estados: ver tabela na página A4

RUY MESQUITA
Diretor responsável

Julio Mesquita (1891-1927)   *Julio de Mesquita Filho (1927-1969)*   ANO 119   **TERÇA-FEIRA**   Nº 38.142   *Francisco Mesquita (1927-1969)*   *Julio de Mesquita Neto (1969-1996)*
SÃO PAULO, 24 DE MARÇO DE 1998

Inferno na mata – *O fogo que consome a floresta amazônica em Roraima avança em Apiaú, o maior centro agrícola da região; a principal causa dos incêndios são as queimadas e, segundo o Inpe, 13% da área do Estado já foi destruída pelas chamas*   Pág. A13

Nomeação de Serra provoca crise com PFL

O senador Guilherme Palmeira, contrariado com a escolha de político de peso do PSDB, diz que seu partido deve reavaliar as indicações para outros ministérios; ACM adota tom conciliador

A escolha do senador José Serra (PSDB-SP) para o Ministério da Saúde deixou contrariados políticos do PFL, partido que apóia o governo Fernando Henrique Cardoso. O fato de Serra chegar com prestígio à Esplanada dos Ministérios levou o senador Guilherme Palmeira (PFL-AL) a lamentar a ремоnоi tomado pela reforma ministerial. "O PFL vai reavaliar suas indicações para outros ministérios, houve mudança de critérios", disse Palmeira. O partido pretende indicar nomes apenas para uma fase de transição, até o início do provável novo mandato de FHC. O presidente do Congresso, senador Antônio Carlos Magalhães (PFL-BA), retornou à ativa na política e até elogiou Serra. ACM desconhece a revolta de alguns líderes nacionais do PFL, que ficaram de procurá-lo hoje. Serra já escolheu, a uma semana de sua posse, o maior desafio para a nova função: evitar o desperdício. Outras prioridades são melhorar o atendimento para pessoas que não têm plano de saúde, criar programas para crianças carentes com menos de 1 ano de idade e dar maior atenção aos portadores de doenças permanentes. O presidente Fernando Henrique está em reunião com o ministro do Trabalho, com vistas ao programa contra o desemprego. Sem a definição dessa nova estrutura, a confirmação oficial de Paulo Paiva no Planejamento e de Sérgio Cutolo no Trabalho foi adiada.   Págs. A6 e A5

Rompido o monopólio de linhas de ônibus

Os serviços de ônibus entre cidades e Estados ganharam ontem novas regras, que permitirão a concorrência entre empresas, eliminando o antigo monopólio de rotas. O presidente Fernando Henrique Cardoso assinou decreto regulamentando as licitações para novas linhas, além dos direitos e obrigações das concessionárias e dos passageiros. De acordo com prazo estabelecido pelo Tribunal de Contas da União, as duas primeiras licitações só deveriam ocorrer dentro de pelo menos 30 dias, para ser possível a avaliação da demanda dessas rotas. O ministro dos Transportes, Eliseu Padilha, afirmou que, com esse decreto, o setor rodoviário está "totalmente aberto". Um grupo econômico fica proibido de explorar, por meio de empresas diferentes, uma mesma linha. Ainda não há previsão para a abertura da concorrência com as empresas que atuam nas ligações entre as capitais, as linhas mais lucrativas.   Pág. B1

Brasil perde o Oscar para filme holandês

O Que É Isso, Companheiro?, do Brasil, perdeu ontem à noite, em Los Angeles, o Oscar de melhor filme estrangeiro de 97 para *Character*, da Holanda, na grande festa do cinema de Hollywood. A derrota do filme do diretor Bruno Barreto foi uma surpresa. Os melhores atores são os autores de *Melhor É Impossível*: Helen Hunt e Jack Nicholson. O melhor ator coadjuvante é Robin Williams. *Titanic* conquistou vários prêmios. O site NetEstado (www.estadao.com.br) traz os resultados completos.   Pág. A14

NOTAS E INFORMAÇÕES

O ministro Carlos Albuquerque foi vítima de um estilo de governo que deixa solto no ar o ministro que não tem peso político próprio. O Ministério do presidente FHC não oferece ambiente para "técnicos". "Sai o clínico geral, entra o cirurgião", na pág. A3

Yeltsin volta e demite todo o ministério

O presidente russo, Boris Yeltsin, demitiu ontem todo o ministério, surpreendendo os meios políticos locais, que não esperavam mudanças repentinas no seu retorno ao Kremlin, depois de dez dias de ausência por motivos de saúde. A saída do primeiro-ministro Viktor Chernomyrdin, que estava havia seis anos à frente do governo, causou rebuliço na Bolsa de Moscou, que caiu 10% no início do pregão. Yeltsin nomeou Serguei Kiriyenko primeiro-ministro interino.   Pág. A18

Kuerten vence Medvedev no torneio Lipton

Gustavo Kuerten, o Guga, derrotou ontem o ucraniano Andrei Medvedev por 6/2, 4/6 e 7/6 (7/5) e classificou-se para as oitavas-de-final do torneio Lipton de tênis. Hoje ele volta à quadra para enfrentar o alemão Nicolas Kiefer. A surpresa da rodada foi a derrota de Pete Sampras para o sul-africano Wayne Ferreira por 0/6, 7/6 (8/6) e 6/3. O resultado poderá custar a Sampras a liderança do ranking, disputada agora por Petr Korda, Marcelo Rios e Greg Rusedski.

Pesquisa prevê segundo turno em São Paulo

Pesquisa de intenção de voto realizada pelo Instituto Vox Populi aponta a possibilidade de a escolha do governador de São Paulo ser decidida apenas no segundo turno. Paulo Maluf (PPB) aparece em primeiro lugar, com 33%. O governador Mário Covas (PSDB), que ainda faz mistério sobre a sua candidatura, é o segundo colocado, com 13%. Num empate técnico, Francisco Rossi (PDT) aparece com 12%, Marta Suplicy (PT) e Luiza Erundina (PSB) têm 9% cada.   Pág. A6

Descontos nas tarifas aéreas são limitados

A anunciada redução de preços nas tarifas aéreas de algumas companhias não está beneficiando o consumidor de forma ampla. Ao contrário dos descontos na Ponte Aérea, as tarifas reduzidas para outras rotas valem apenas para poucos lugares nos aviões. Um programa de computador faz o gerenciamento de rentabilidade dos vôos e determina quantos vagas estão disponíveis para cada faixa de preço.   Viagem

Vitória do talento – *A atriz Helen Hunt recebe o troféu, em Los Angeles, depois de ser derrotada Judi Dench, Julie Christie, Kate Winslet e Helena Bonham Carter, na grande noite de Hollywood*

Revolvendo a história – *O corpo de uma menina de 10 anos é uma das 60 múmias retiradas de ruínas romanas no Egito pela arqueóloga Françoise Dunand, da Universidade de Estrasburgo*   Pág. A16

- Agricultor quer o mesmo tratamento dos sem-terra   Pág. A12
- Os muito ricos da Ásia perdem bilhões na crise   Pág. B12
- PF desativa suposta bomba no Congresso   Pág. A9
- BNDES negocia verba de US$ 1 bi para área social   Pág. A15
- Zagallo usa treino para tirar a última dúvida   Páginas E1
- Palmeiras disputa vaga hoje contra o Botafogo   Pág. E2

Coleção Castelo Rá-Tim-Bum Estadão.

TEMPO

SUAS CONTAS

HOJE   128 páginas

sapphire and diamond brooch representing the Argentinean blue and white striped flag. This jewel reached an amazing price at an auction; thus, the story and illustration appeared on the first page. Evita was the very embodiment of the anima (as Carmen Miranda was for Brazil in the same time).[5] Anima and woman are certainly different realities, but when there is a collective complex in the psychological integration of the archetype of the anima by men, certain women incarnate those qualities in concrete terms, at the cost of their personal psychologies and even their lives. The brooch corresponds to a phase when Evita had unparalleled power and was the queen of the poor, before whom she paraded Dior gala gowns and promised social upgrading and redemption if only they voted for Perón. The national flag, meaning both the country and its people, was turned into a jewel to be worn at the breast as if to express the unconscious fact that populist politics was ruled by the anima and her style.

The false promises of demagogic leaders can be wrought into a piece of jewelry, but is the newspaper not also an illusion? Are we not letting ourselves be deceived daily if we just accept passively all that is printed and given us to be swallowed with our coffee and cornflakes? If we base our perceptions on what the media give us, if we espouse collective values, would there remain an inner, uncontaminated standpoint to which we could cling? What then is a newspaper? What is our conscious, and unconscious, relationship to it, and what has the newspaper got to do with individuation at all?

We Jungians have indeed an important task: to develop concepts or tools in order to check whether new contents are emerging from the depths of the collective unconscious. Marie-Louise von Franz—in the last seminar she gave at the Jung Institute in Zurich, in 1980—explained to us that the image of the queen living in a castle in a faraway island meant that the feminine archetype would slowly rise like a new star in the horizon.[6] And she warned us to watch carefully for such appearances. I believe we have to develop this kind of antenna to detect what is new, what is coming up from the depths. How do we measure it? How do we identify it? How do we distinguish genuine from virtual contents, permanent from transient ones? We have to come to that understanding ourselves and with our patients and culture.

Something is taking shape on the front page of the newspaper. It is certainly a collective endeavor. Maybe it cannot be called a precise name; maybe we do not know what it is all about. If we do not catch that, we remain stuck to the surface of what is already changing within the realm of collective consciousness. Perhaps we might help these contents that are moving upward really to come up, like a birth. Jung asserted that there are parts of the unconscious that impose themselves to be assimilated. It is not just a question of personal effort, like fishing these hidden contents up—they are coming up by themselves. This is a very Jungian, not at all Freudian, approach. And what is unconscious? Everything that is yet unknown to us, everything we ignore. But we know there is something there, because of its indirect expression and because perhaps part of it is moving toward us.

In definite periods of history this phenomenon becomes especially detectable. We fantasize that something of the sort will happen in the new millennium. Nobody can tell, but the sign of Aquarius undeniably points to that. We have been living under the rule of Pisces, as Jung commented in *Aion*, the two fishes going in opposite directions.[7] That is dualism: East and West, body and spirit, capitalism and communism, monotheism and polytheism, right and wrong, normal and abnormal. What then is the image of Aquarius? A man, the Waterman, holding a cup in each hand. With one he collects water that falls from the sky, which then is poured into the second cup. What could that mean? He works with the unconscious. Jung believed that in the third millennium, ruled by a new fundamental archetype, humanity could learn how to do that work. Instead of opposing the unconscious, we will work with it, thereby allowing us to discover healing, creative, and transforming powers hitherto unavailable to us. So the task is to collect fresh water and pour it into another recipient. When we note a dream we collect celestial water. When we connect meaningfully to archetypal images we gather water from the unconscious and then transfer it to the other vessel, which is our science, our profession, our way of doing things. In this way perhaps we can unlock new dimensions in our growth and development.

I think this is a very Jungian quest, a truly modern myth, and in this sense I share the images expressed on the front page of the newspaper.

I also believe that such a precious tool as Jungian psychology should not be kept only for clinical psychotherapy. We have to deal with the injuries of the world around us and have to test to what degree our discipline can be effective. People criticize Jung by saying that he was mystical, but he only talked about things that he could observe and experience. Some people say they cannot understand what is meant by individuation, the transcendent function, or anima. Yet these are very elementary ideas, if only one is able to translate them into understandable terms. These ideas can certainly be used to work with our human family and environment. This is our challenge, and I firmly believe we can meet it. We could come to a precise definition of the contribution we make: opening up new angles of perception of meaning.

CHAPTER 2

Soul Making in the New World

We Americans, whether from North, Central, or South America, have to come into contact with the ancestral soul of our land and try to know more about it than just what we learned in elementary school. We were taught that the Americas were discovered. If you say you have discovered something you might be right, or you may have fallen into ethnocentrism. In this case, it is implied that if something is not known by you, and you are the center of the world, that thing does not exist. After traveling to the United States, I could go back home to Brazil and say that I have discovered Texas, or a whole university, and perhaps I should take possession of it because I discovered it. In the way it has been traditionally told, our history begins with this very egocentric attitude that the Western Hemisphere did not exist and was not included in the common understanding of humanity.

We know today that the Americas, from Alaska to Patagonia, were inhabited by eighty million people at the turn of the sixteenth century, one fifth of the planet's population, which was then four hundred million.[1] It is high time for us to think more deeply about what happened to those eighty million ancestors of ours. We should be able to grasp and develop the idea that those people had been creating soul on these continents for the last thirty thousand years. But we learn at school that soul was brought to America by its discoverers, because they looked at the native people and thought they were soulless. The Jesuits wrote letters in 1549 that these pagan people were in between animals and humans. This observation soon started a theological debate in the Iberian Peninsula in which scholars would argue what kinds of beings those creatures were, if they belonged to creation at all, if they had been made by God or the devil. So the main point of the "discovery" project was to give a soul to the Indians.

When I was collecting old images for my research, I came across a highly symbolical engraving by the German naturalist Carl von Martius, printed in 1856.[2] A gigantic tree is encircled by a mandala of Indians, while two European scientists watch close by. This image conveys the whole idea. Our ancestors are the hidden roots; the trunk is the joined genetic pool of Indian, white, and black men and women. The branches are our history. In the North they received more sunlight and water, so they grew fast. In the South, so much was taken from the ground that half of the American Tree could not develop evenly, and that we call underdevelopment. I am one who has been trying for decades to understand this problem by going back to the wounded part of the tree, believing we can only overcome underdevelopment if the tree grows in the right way and fulfills its inherent potential.

I will tell you how this research began and how this train of thought originated. My personal task was to bring together two different schools of thinking: one extroverted, the social sciences; and the other introverted, depth psychology. I would not abandon my first training in the social sciences for the sake of becoming a pure analytical psychologist, so I had to make a marriage between these two currents—and I am still working on it.

In the beginning I was very much interested in outside realities as such. In 1978 I was invited to join a team of anthropologists to spend time in an Indian reserve in the state of São Paulo, which, as the rest of the country or the whole of the Americas, had been previously inhabited by Indians who subsequently lost their lands. Presently, all these Indians are living in poverty. They were forced to abandon their traditional ways and now they work as paid laborers. Our task was to interview them using a socio-economic questionnaire dealing with crops, wages, and hours of labor. One particular man, called Jasone, from the Terena tribe, caught my attention. He was a very centered, quiet, but strong man. After going through my economic questions, all of a sudden I asked him if he remembered any of his dreams. To my astonishment and contentment, he told me this most amazing dream, which could have been the dream of any Indian over the last five hundred years: "I went to the old Guarani cemetery at the reserve, and there I saw a large cross. Some white men arrived and nailed me upside down to the cross. They left and I remained desperate. I woke up very frightened."

This dream gave meaning to my work and set me to do a never-ending research. My book *Indian Mirror: The Making of the Brazilian Soul,* is an attempt to understand this dream.[3] Why would an Indian be nailed upside down to the cross by white men? And what does it mean?

I will now bring you a series of interconnected ideas, so we can hopefully understand this dream progressively. What happened in the sixteenth century—the conquest of the Americas and the meeting of two parts of humanity, European Catholics and native Indians—was such a portentous event that nowadays it would be like meeting extra-terrestrials from Venus or Jupiter. We are still not completely aware of what this meeting implied and how it ended up in ethnocide. The eighty million people present when the encounter took place were, in the course of one century, reduced to twenty-five million. Brazil alone had ten million Indians in 1500, when the Portuguese first landed on the coast. Today there are fewer than three hundred thousand individuals scattered around. Five centuries ago there were more than 1,000 cultures, and that meant hundreds of different languages, mythological systems, religions, kinship arrangements, implements, architectures, rituals, bodies of knowledge, views of the world. All these human achievements have been reduced today to 170 cultures. The rest is lost forever.

When Christian Europeans disembarked on Indian lands, two great archetypal opposites met. But the opposition was so extreme and the psychological attitude of the time was such that there was no attempt at integrating them, or this process would have the meaning that it acquired for us today. One opposite destroyed the other rather than both alchemically transforming for the sake of arriving at a third configuration.

When we, the Americans, were born as a people, there was both a birth and an abortion. A new people was born, but a new human possibility was aborted. This tragic deed, which has for centuries remained unnamed and unexamined, has to do with a specific kind of relationship between men and women that was established in the New World.

Only males crossed the ocean to conquer South America. In North America it was different, because there were couples fleeing religious persecution. The contact between the British and the Indians was somehow different, although no less destructive. The Portuguese and Spanish *conquistadores* were adventurers, scoundrels, survivors of shipwrecks, mercenaries, and all sorts of disqualified types, together with a few nobles and tradesmen. They were all seeking quick fortune, a new life, and a way to re-enter society as winners or to escape the reach of the terrible Catholic Inquisition. (Many were on the black list.)

The whole adventure was linked to old ideas and fantasies that Paradise existed in this part of the Earth, or the land of the fearsome Amazons, or the Eldorado, the golden man who knew the secrets of inexhaustible mines. There were also morbid fantasies about people who ate human flesh or had different bodies—one eye, a hairy skin, strange sexual organs. Imaginations of this kind refer, of course, only to the European collective unconscious, having absolutely nothing to do with the new realities found in the Western Hemisphere.

The "discoverers" were very phallic, in the sense that they had a keen capacity or a will to penetrate into the unknown, to cross the indomitable ocean, the dangerous rain forest, and to conquer Indian women. All these newcomers from Europe brought with them a fantastic new achievement called ego consciousness. This differentiated part of the psyche, structured upon rationality, had been slowly maturing since the dark times of the Middle Ages, when an individual had to submit and adjust himself to a dogmatic view of the world and give up any personal attempt to gather proofs of what was declared to be the universal truth.

In the sixteenth century, Renaissance men had discovered perspective, anatomy, the blood circulatory system, gunpowder, powerful sailing boats, geographical and celestial charts, the press, cannons, the astrolabe, and the compass. While Leonardo da Vinci and Michelangelo were painting their wonderful images, architects were inventing new urban concepts, and the neoplatonists were expanding psychological dimensions. Descartes's famous philosophical statement, "I think, therefore I am," corresponds to the birth of rationality as the new ruling principle of collective consciousness. Rationality was being born. It was fresh, new, and full of energy.

Christian men were therefore ego-centered, and they felt an inner pressure to expand, to act, to influence the world, to let this rational consciousness run free as wild horses and take over the whole universe. They were eager to conquer space and to shape up new human beings similar to their own countenance, as in the myth of Genesis.

Psychologically speaking, these European men wanted to be like God and make a new creation. The eighty million Indians who had been for ages living in the conquered territory had a different psychology, the main difference being the absence of a sharply differentiated individual ego consciousness. Theirs was what we call today a non-rational consciousness, because it did not operate through logical separations; instead, it worked by apprehension of great ensembles, what today we call the holistic mind. For the European, time was a straight line, an arrow shooting forever forward. For the Aztecs, the Mayas, the Incas, the Tupi, the Guarani, or all the Indians all over the land, time was circular, always returning in cycles to the point of departure.

For Indian consciousness there are no clashing opposites. Body and spirit are different manifestations of the same unitarian entity. One always reflects and affects the other. Inside and outside are the same; only their visibility changes. Sacred and profane are not clearly demarcated but endlessly inter-penetrating each other. Men can be always strong and soft, and women can always be soft and strong, both being equivalent in the order of things both socially and transcendentally. The Godhead is male and female or neither, is good and bad or neither. The psyche, as Jung noted in his study on projection, spreads over trees, rivers, animals, plants, celestial bodies, people, and objects. Nature is totally alive, and it is sacred.

Indian consciousness developed a special attitude toward knowledge, in the sense that it did not require the destruction of the object. Contemplation was more important than dissection. Categories and systems of classification were not mutually exclusive, and they allowed for a vast array of empirical observations covering our fields of astronomy, botany, anatomy, medicine, agronomy, mythology, social organization, law, ethics, diplomacy, aesthetics, technology, religion, and etiquette.

In the course of the last thirty thousand years or so, those eighty million people had solved all the fundamental questions of humanity: how to survive, in the first place; how to procreate, establish kinship relations, and raise children; how to form a community with rules of behavior and a system of authority; how to build houses, to hunt, to gather or produce food, and cook it in appropriate vessels; how to find water and create fire; how to cure diseases and alleviate pain; how to understand the workings of nature; how to find beauty, meaning, and pleasure in life; how to avoid suffering; and how to accept death.

When the two different parts of humanity we are talking about met, a powerful crossed projection took place. An image comes to mind of two birds flying in opposite directions—one coming from the East, the other from the West. They meet when they cross each other in the sky. They mate for a brief moment and then fly away from each other. This is, for me, the image of what I have called a crossed projection. Europeans projected onto the native people their own shadow, consisting of everything good Christians were not willing to acknowledge as being also part of their human reality—in ecclesiastical terminology, the seven deadly sins. Projection was then the automatic, quick, and easy way of getting rid of all this uncomfortable stuff that could sometimes create a sensation of bad conscience and would, in religious terms, lead to assumption of guilt, confession, repentance, and punishment before absolution was given as an act of God's mercifulness.

It would take centuries for white people to recognize that they were greedy, unjust, cruel, sadistic, hypocritical, envious of their neighbors' spouses and property, murderous, insatiable, perverse, insisting on their undisputed right to have everything they wanted, especially to be free from an ethical obligation to follow both the civil and the dogmatic law. On Sunday morning they would go to mass, but all the rest of the time they would indulge in their shadows' inclinations. In Portugal and Spain there were civil and criminal tribunals and a code of laws, besides the dictatorial Inquisition, which was autocratically above the law. In Central Europe, Luther, Calvin, and Zwingli were pointing their angry fingers at the unbridled Catholic shadow—loss of ethics, commerce of indulgences, usury, religious hypocrisy. The church feared the accusations raised by the Protestant leaders not only because of a possible loss of power, but because an ugly shadow was progressively being exposed.

In this context, while the movement of the counter-Reformation inaugurated a period of excessive and compensatory austerity soon to be heralded by the Spanish monarch Felipe II, the pope Alexander VI proclaimed a bombastic bill declaring that there was no sin below the equator. This single statement suffices for us to understand the dynamics of the collective shadow seeking for a good authoritative pretext to be projected. In Jungian terms, the papal bill meant that below the equator—that is, in the vast expanse of land occupied by the Portuguese and partly by the Spanish—the archetypal shadow was allowed to run free without inhibition, control, or punishment. In one word: the conquerors were allowed to live out whatever they pleased.

As the highest ecclesiastical authority had legitimately entitled them to conquer the land and subdue its inhabitants, they could also enslave them, steal their women, and through the Jesuit missionaries (their allies), catechize them, forcing them under the threat of death to abandon their religion and adopt the Catholic faith. The projection that justified such procedures was that the Indians were lazy, promiscuous, guilty of nakedness, apolitical, agnostic, and soulless—all that the Catholic shadow was secretly desiring to be and beginning to act out.

The European projection was double-binded. On the one side, there was the projection of evil and Hell. The Indians were regarded as Lucifer's offspring, in another act of rebellion against God, who could not have created such bestial creatures. Women, especially, were seen through the image of the serpent, if not that of Lilith. They were regarded as insidious, false, and dangerous beings whose destiny would be to be curbed, disciplined, chastised, and baptized. The Jesuits wanted to turn them into nuns. The Indian shamans, in particular, were seen as the concrete embodiment of Satan.

On the other hand, there was also the projection of Paradise, based on fantasies dating from the Middle Ages and the empirical fact that tropical nature looked exuberantly lush, with candidly naked, childish people walking around at leisure. Paradise was the garden of the children of God, a virginal place in which the newcomers were also free from the burden of the shadow. They were the beloved ones to whom all the garden's delights would be granted at no cost, and there was no talk about the Fall.

Portuguese men crossed the ocean and left their wives back home. Their women were pious, dominated, and repressed. They wore black robes for most of the time and, following their husbands' departure, they would adopt the role of widows of living spouses who went away never to return or only many years later. When these men, freed from family and ethical ties, met naked Indian women, the complete opposite of the kind of women they knew, they immediately projected upon them the image of Eve. And they wanted to have that Eve, because they saw themselves as Adam. But that masculine archetype would not be extended to the Indian males. In a smart twist of mythological logic, the men were seen exclusively as slaves, not even as rivals. Eve would be their playmate and companion; Indian males would be kept out of the garden.

Indian healers all over the world work with the powers of the unconscious to bring about cures for all kinds of illnesses or psychological possessions. When shamans realized what these white men had in mind and what they were actually doing, they warned all members of the tribe not to have any contact with them, because baptismal water, beads, mirrors, iron knives, combs, clothes, axes, and scissors would kill them. The Jesuits, who pursued as maniacs the goal of global conversion, regarded the shamans as their worst enemies, because they mirrored to the priests the worst part of their own shadow, namely, the burning desire to perform miracles and control spiritual powers. It is historically recorded that the missionaries were often two-faced and deceived the Indians with tricks to mesmerize them. For example, they said that holy water healed any kind of disease or that the touch of their hands had spiritual power to cause physical alterations over the body, objects, or the waves of the sea. The missionaries, as their work progressed, got so inflated that they had a secret identification with the apostles. Not only that, as time went by and they grew impatient to see all of Brazil converted to Christianity, they reached higher, unheard-of levels of identification with Christ himself, and even with the Holy Ghost. So they could not tolerate shamans who claimed to have clairvoyance and contact with the spirit world. Onto them they threw the image of the devil himself, therefore justifying their argument in favor of their enslavement or elimination.

So this was the Eastern bird, the bird that flew toward the garden of Paradise or the abysses of Hell, following its own route of mythical projections. The Western bird followed a completely different path, and it is absolutely necessary that we understand this counter-projection.

When the Aztecs saw Hernán Cortez and his powerful army landing in Mexico in 1519, with their fantastic sailing vessels, their shining helmets, their leather boots, their spears, beards and cannons, horses and dogs, they immediately projected onto the newly disembarked *conquistadores* the image of their god Quetzalcoatl, who had once fled Mexico going east through the sea and who, one day—time being cyclical—would return to rescue humanity. So when they saw in astonishment the Spaniards in all their power approaching the shore, what they saw was their savior coming back as promised, bringing with him the hope of good times to come. They courteously welcomed those who were soon to destroy them.

In Brazil too there was much messianism. The Guarani Indians in particular believed that unknown men would one day appear from the sea to take the whole tribe, who would have wandered for thousands of miles to reach the shore, to the Land Without Evil, a mythical place where men were relieved from the burdens of terrestrial life. A similar projection took place upon Portuguese sailors, who actually wanted to save no one, except their own selves.

How could such different birds meet at all? Were they possibly attracted to each other on account of their very difference? Could they ever mate and stay together? They could not. These projections, as we have seen, were mutually exclusive. They cannot coexist. It is impossible, a contradiction in terms. The first projection was stronger than the Indian one but not by itself. Intrinsically both had the same strength. But the European projection was supported by material power, and that means gunpowder, vessels, the Soldiers of Christ, the Portuguese crown, and also by religious and symbolic weapons as baptism, the cross, and the mass.

Remember the dream? It depicts the most powerful weapon of all: the cross. The cross was the first symbol to be imposed on the Indian psyche. They were made to revere and adore it, when in reality they had to carry it through labor, humiliation, and endless suffering. The cross was like a dagger, because whenever it was erected as a wooden monument of the conquest, as a white man's erect phallus penetrating conquered lands, it painfully pierced the ancestral soul to death.

The presence of the Christian cross meant that the Indians had to abandon their culture, their mythology, their religion, and their gods. The pope made a public statement in 2000 asking for pardon, acknowledging that the Catholic church and the missionaries who worked during colonial times for the conversion of souls in the Americas, in China, Japan, India, and the African continent had regrettably done a terribly destructive work. This was the first time the church recognized that it had no right and no reason to say that the Indians were unable to conceive, revere, and believe in a divinity. Church authorities have awkwardly begun to ask for forgiveness, but we must realize that it is not enough, nor commensurate to all the wrongs done, to declare repentance. Christians know, when their sins are at stake, that a deep ethical transformation is required, not just a hurried confession of guilt. Something else has to be done, a more mature and responsible consciousness has to be developed onward at an increasingly deeper ethical level.

The cross is the central symbol of Christianity. It represents the idea that one part of us has to die nailed to it. It is also the meeting of the opposites and the resolution of the tension created by them. To be crucified is to be torn apart between the vertical and the horizontal pull. The tension grows so unbearably strong that one dies at the heaven-earth connection. According to Christ, this is an absolute necessity for us—to be aware that we are only the children of God and that we live in two realms, the earthly one and Our Father's realm. So every genuine Christian has to be crucified sooner or later. And that means precisely that until that deep climax of inner psychological and spiritual change is reached, we have to carry the weight of our sins, or the cross of our shadow upon our shoulders. This is no easy task and corresponds to what Jung has called the sacrifice of the ego—or egocide, a term coined by David Rosen—in other words, the individuation process.[4] Nobody can do it for us. There is no easy way out. Each one of us has to live our own version of the passion of Christ as he carried the cross of humanity's sins upon his shoulders. That is painful. It surely makes you suffer more than you can stand. But it makes you realize who you really are, with no persona, no disguise, no apologies, nor justifications. And until you achieve that you cannot be transformed, and you cannot contact the Self.

The cross is a wonderful and profound symbol, but it has absolutely nothing to do with Indian psychology, religion, and mythology. Christ never said that there was an easy way to do it and that one can make another one carry the cross for him. But this is exactly what the "discoverers" did. It was as if they said: "We do not have to carry it. We will make the Indians do it for us. They, not us, are the sinners. They are the children of the devil; we are not. They are promiscuous and lazy. They, not us, lack virtue. So let them carry the burden, and we will crucify them in the end."

I am looking for the day when an artist, or a child, will paint this image, the fundamental image for the understanding of the soul of the Americas: an Indian being crucified. This exact image appeared in a Terena Indian's dream, but there the situation was still worse: he was crucified upside down. To grasp the meaning of this we have to plunge into deep and muddy waters.

Where else do we find this upside-down crucifixion? We have an instance of that in the Tarot, in the arcane called The Hanged Man, a figure that indicates an imminent process of transformation and reversal of the prevailing situation. As far as Christian iconography is concerned, there is only one image of this kind, and that is the crucifixion of St. Peter. In his time, that was the worst sacrifice, because all blood would flow to the head. According to Gnostic tradition, the image means that the Anthropos, or the archetypal essential man, fell to the earth head first. The way man comes to the earth and enters embodied, dense reality is upside down, reversing his prior transcendental nature into bodily existence. Babies are born in that symbolic position. People have to enter this world in an inverted position because this is the way to acquire true knowledge of what we are—simple, transient beings and not the rulers of the universe. To understand this symbol we have to turn our consciousness upside down, like in a Zen teaching, or in a Jungian teaching. Everything you believed will be reversed. The notion you had of yourself will be reversed. This is what to be crucified upside down means.

But why on earth must an Indian be crucified upside down? Indians were already upside down from their beginning. It suffices to consider the style of consciousness they developed, in which nothing is simply this or that, but this *and* that at the same time. Their religion did not speak of crosses, because they were not split between the archetypal opposites as we have become through the development of the Western hybrids. They did not have to work the tension of the opposites, because opposites were not in tense disharmony in them. The real tension was between us and them—created by us and not by them—because we were greedy, but they opened their arms. So the cross is not an apt symbol for an Indian individuation process. It is a symbol for our psychology, and it has been a dirty historical trick to make the Indians carry the cross for us. Asking for forgiveness now is simply not enough.

Going in another direction, we can also look at the situation we have been trying to describe from another angle, and that would be an analysis of our founding father and mother. As a new people, we Latin Americans were born as a hybrid product of different kinds of men and women. Our ancestral father is a white man with a phallic rational ego, and our ancestral great mother an Indian, later a black, and then a white woman. Portuguese men were sexually attracted to Indian and African women, whereas in North America the Quakers were not. That makes an enormous difference in what concerns the soul. The Portuguese approached these Eve-like women and procreated with them. We are the offspring of this mating, and a big problem was created, although historians have never recognized it at the psychological level. I am talking about the problem of identity, the existential question of knowing who we are.

The first Latin Americans had mixed blood, but they also had a mixed psyche. We know today that in order to develop a clear identity people need to identify projectively, at least a bit, with their mothers and fathers or their surrogates. A point then is reached in one's psychological development in which it is possible to say "this is me. I come from these roots, which in turn come from other roots." So I can place myself in this stream of time. I can locate myself historically. I know where I came from. I know my unique ways, and because I know my origins I can love and work and envision a future. You cannot do it if you do not know from where you came. This is precisely what underdevelopment is all about. A country in this situation cannot see itself as utopia, because it gets lost in non-being.

These first Americans were nobodies. Little insignificant nobodies. They were bastards, illegitimate children, hybrids, *mestizos, criollos*. What would happen if the father decided to take his bastard children to Spain or to Portugal for a visit? Many in fact did. Indians and American-born youths were looked at in Europe as little more than monkeys or parrots, strange birds to be exhibited in the open square in front of the church or as curious items in museum displays. They would also actually be engaged to entertain the French court at palace festivities in Rouen or Versailles.

Sometimes these white Christian fathers sailed back to Portugal or Spain, taking their children with them. These sons and daughters would then be in their father's land, but there was no place for them in the European society. In the case of a son, he could not join the military forces nor enter the academy and become a teacher. He could not open a shop to establish himself as a tradesman, nor could he work with money, gold, brazil-wood, or other colonial export goods. He would just have to stay quiet and invisible at the outer fringes of a closely structured hierarchical society. In his father's land he would be a pariah, an expatriate. Father's land was definitely no fatherland. This is the occult tragic dimension of a difficult process of broken identity following the paternal line.

These first Americans could not receive from the father a sense of legitimacy and belonging. They were not introduced to the world by the father, who failed to perform his archetypal duty, to bring his children to the world's doorway and explain them their legitimate right to belong there and how it works. The father says: "Dear son, dear daughter, I bring you to this point and here I bid farewell. This is the way the world functions. If you behave in this way you will succeed; if you behave in that way you will fail. Take my word with you and go into the world. You are a legitimate person. You do not have to feel inferior. Do not ever lower your head. Trust and love yourself."

This is what a father does. He explains and passes on the rules he got from his father and his ancestors. We, in the New World, have a pathological and immoral father. How can such a shadowy figure establish ethical laws? How can he tell his children to follow any established moral or legal code if he himself was transgressing them every day of his life? That is the origin of our collective father problem.

But we also have a mother problem. The mother archetype moves every woman who embodies it to protect and love her children as they are and for what they are, and to nurture and not only to feed them, helping a sense of inner value to develop. I am worth something, because I have seen my mother's eyes looking at me with pleasure. I know that she is happy with her creation and that I have personal worth. If you cannot acquire a sense of selfhood through your mother, then you do not know who you are, and you do not know whether you are worth anything at all.

These nobodies who were the first Americans were unsure about their identity and their worth. What prevented Indian mothers from being the traditionally wonderful mothers they had been? I have observed the relationship between Zoro Indian women and infants—the way they carry their babies attached to their bodies while going out to work, how they give their breasts entirely to them for intermittent feeding alternating with sleep as the baby pleases. They give their bodies entirely to the suckling and are in no way exempted from having to do daily heavy work, like crossing rivers over tree trunks and going into the bush to plant or to collect roots. After one year or so, when the babies can already walk, they are detached from their total intimacy with their mothers' bodies, also because the mothers might be having other children by then. I have observed that these young children accept the change in a tranquil way, without regression, without making scenes to manipulate the mothers to take them back to their bosoms. It can only be because while the babies were nursing, the mothers' breasts were entirely theirs, without any limits, even while sleeping on the mothers' bellies the whole night. So children learn how to progress to the successive steps of their development. That is why little Indian boys and girls are so responsible and mature. They had to—for necessity—be able to survive by themselves as soon as possible. And it is possible.

I wonder why there has never been psychological research comparing the Indian way of rearing children with our modern ways. It would be shocking to our sense of superiority to realize that in many essential aspects of life they have much more wisdom than we do. And then, what would we do with our five-century-old prejudices? Maybe this is the reason why such a research has never been done. Having been able to observe the mother-child relationship for a good period of time while living with the Zoro Indians of Northwestern Brazil, I came to the conclusion that theoreticians like Melanie Klein would have to dismiss a large part of what they maintain to be true. Indian mothers do not have a bad breast at all. This seems to be simply a European psychological projection, or fantasy, turned into scientific truth. Indian women at least, in their proper cultural environment, are apt carriers of the mother archetype.

What prevented them from transmitting to their offspring the sense of love and worth so essential for acquiring a clear awareness of identity, ancestry, and future possibilities? The root of the problem was a specific kind of relationship between men and women whereby women were not allowed to fulfill their task because they were psychologically devalued. This is not a personal handicap stemming from individual shortcomings but indeed a collective cultural and historical problem determined by the way the masculine principle of rational consciousness overpowered and ultimately destroyed the feminine principle of soul psychology. The European way of thinking could not recognize that Indian consciousness was just as valuable as itself, albeit from a different standpoint. It had to underrate the other. And this is the tragic dimension of our birth as a people.

We were born as the strange fruit of a particular tree in which one sap was in disharmony with the other. The masculine sap, or energy, would say: "Indian women have very little to contribute. Let us just stay with their bodies, thighs, hair, lips, vaginas, uteruses, breasts, working hands... that is enough. Let us keep a little bit of their cooking abilities, their resistance. Let us adopt their hammocks, their clay pots, their basketry, their weaving, and their straw mats. Let us borrow their fathers' weapons and their agricultural skills. The rest—their language, their prayers, their songs, their feelings and points of view, the stories they tell—is all rubbish."

The practical result of this masculine attitude was that Indian women were the first housemaids in the Americas. They were soon in the sixteenth century forced to clean the Jesuits' houses and churches. Their challenge was quite different than that befalling their fathers, brothers, husbands, and sons, because they had to open their legs for the invaders. They had to chose between being raped or being baptized, then mating with white males, and ultimately being expelled from their original tribes. Indian women all over the continent were following a wise law of nature according to which, for their genes to survive, they had to mate with the conqueror, at the cost of having their souls reduced to nothingness. This was undoubtedly an extreme psychological task, and I say that the feminine voice—the only one entitled to tell this story in all its depth and complexity—has been silenced for the last five hundred years.

Everything we know about the previous stages of our psychological development or the difficult process of building a collective identity has been told by a masculine voice, with a corresponding logic and a particular point of view, which nevertheless was generalized as the overall truth. We must absolutely develop a capacity to listen to a silent speech and imagine a history explained by the feminine soul. How it experienced being raped by the masculine Logos. How it experienced not being allowed to transmit ancient wisdom and a sense of unique worth to the new generations. How it reacted when the innermost nucleus of its being was reduced to ashes. Unless we know this story, we will not be able to understand the soul in the New World.

There is still a profound collective psychological task to be undertaken. The consequences of what happened when the birds of crossed projections met each other have not stopped. Seventy percent of the Brazilian population has Indian and black genes. Genetics is now making important discoveries, such as that there is no such thing as a race, because at the genetic level we are all equal. Genes are the physical carriers of the collective unconscious. So our psychological ancestry is present here and now both in genetic terms as in cultural and psychic conditioning and assimilation. Those who lack Amerindian genes—overseas immigrants, for instance—still are able to feel empathy and ethical commitment. As the ancestral soul is in us and with us, we all carry its pain and the original dissociation between two archetypal principles that affected it from the beginning of our collective journey. The rational and non-rational dimensions of our psyche have not yet come together and until that happens we suffer from arrested individuation.

When I visited College Station, I was excited when David Rosen showed me Texas wildflowers, the bluebonnet and the red Indian paintbrush, lining the highway. We then stopped at a village called Chapel Hill, founded by women in the nineteenth century. We went into the local general store, and there I bought a kitchen towel with the image of a cowboy boot holding a bunch of bluebonnets. The thought came to me that here opposites were meeting. I also got a cigar with a yellow rose in its label. While strolling on the Texas A&M campus, we observed that the psychology building was across from the military science building. This coming together of opposites, whose manifestation we can detect in sometimes very prosaic episodes, actually opens new ways for the mind to work with psychology and the social sciences.

Like a few other colleagues in our field, I use the word *soul* to understand a historical process. Some people feel uncomfortable with this. Sociologists, historians, and anthropologists all resist this approach, claiming that it is neither scientific nor theoretically adequate. However, when we try to bring science and soul together we take a step toward mending what has been torn apart. When we work with soul and education, we re-introduce our founding father and mother. Pragmatism and positivism denied the non-rational mother principle—a mental field with no room for poetry, intuition, magic, spirituality, feeling, images. We Jungians are all for images, more so than for words, because we know images come first and tell more. Word belongs to the father, image to the mother.

Any tiny bit of work that we do in ourselves, or in our profession, if it is oriented by this symbol of unification of opposites is a contribution. It might be a drop of water in the desert, but it might help a new life to keep thriving. In order to do so, we must be in tune with this myth, which to me is the founding myth of the Americas, a *coniunctio oppositorum*, as Jung liked to say, of substances that never fused into each other at the soul level.

Indian women did not fail to perform their archetypal role historically but were prevented from playing that role fully. To the children, the mother represented the defeated and conquered one, and that situation in itself made identification problematic. The natural tendency of children is to identify themselves with something that is successful, that works well, that is rewarding. It is more difficult to identify with a principle, a cause, or an idea that has been defeated. This was the first reason, and the second was that no family was created. The father procreated, but he would not become a husband, and he would not create a solid nucleus of partnership. Usually mother and father help each other to be what they are. Father probably never said, "Listen to what your mother has to say." He would not let mother be mother. In my view, this is the original problem. He never saw her as his equal and never created any kind of soul partnership with her. We have documents in Brazil concerning inheritance in which you can see that John so-and-so was legally married and had so many children by a woman with a Portuguese name. Then there follows a list of twenty children with Indian names, but their mothers are not mentioned. He had children with seven, eight, ten Indian women who where not to be considered his wives. It was not a polygamous marriage, because that was prohibited by the church and by civil law. Moreover, the father would never bring all those women to live with him and establish a household. What can a woman do if she does not have a place for herself? She needs a hearth in which she will cook and around which family life will develop. And she must have control over some territory, which is her household, and this is provided for and protected by the husband. If the man degrades her, as just a body and not his peer, he will not allow her to perform her archetypal task.

The psychological impact of the conquest on Indian men was depression. Indian males were courageous and strong, active, resourceful, and potent men, both physically and psychologically. Because they could not resist armed invasion and enslavement, they got depressed. The first attempt at establishing slavery in Brazil in the sixteenth century, as well as in Mexico, Peru, and the Antilles, was to enslave Indians. Do you know why it did not work? They would rather commit suicide than lose their freedom and dignity. Only captive Africans could endure that, and we still know so little how it worked for them psychologically. They were humiliated and depressed too, but they would not put an end to their lives as the Indians did. We do not have statistics; a precise knowledge of this process is lost forever. We do not know how many killed themselves due to exhaustion or despair or died as a result of European diseases.

The will to die appears when the Self is brutally denied, when there is nothing left. This was the main impact, but today two kinds of Indians remain, at least in Brazil: those still living tribal lives and those who have lost their original community, quite often because they lost their land and their culture. The two groups are in different psychological positions. Those living tribal life know about the so-called civilization. They want some consumer goods and facilities, but they want to keep their tradition because they think it is better. So they are more tranquil in a way, although they are aware that capitalist expansion will ultimately reach them.

Tribal life is one of the best creations of humanity, and we still do not know how to understand or appreciate it. It is so full of wisdom—to my knowledge there is practically no me-mine behavior as far as it is not contaminated by disrupting factors. I have not read one single psychological in-depth study of tribal life. Those who have lost their tribes did it first of all because they lost their territories and their mythology. Without them, they can no longer be Indians, only survivors of a lost past. These individuals fall into an abyss: a complex psychological state, because they no longer know who they are and do not know who they want to become. It so happens that they end up coming into contact with and assimilating the worst aspects of white society. They begin to lie and play tricks, and so their shadow grows in unusual ways. They take to drinking, lose their previous ingenuity, and cannot be trusted anymore for what they say. They change their prior patterns of loyalty. Some colleagues doing field research have gone through complex situations on that account. After working for twenty years with Indians undergoing acculturation they would find out that for no apparent reason the Indians would no longer trust them. For those still living the traditional communal life it is also difficult, but they have old, solid roots to sustain them. Either way, it is a taxing human challenge.

When I was studying in Zurich I once consulted Marie-Louise von Franz about these problems, asking her what she thought would be the future of our Indians. She closed her eyes and as in a visionary state of mind she said: "They will disappear; only a few of them will remain, and they will be like a spiritual reserve for mankind." A spiritual reserve—we must go to them, so we can learn how to revive our own spirit.

Our hope is that depth psychology, making us deal with material that has not yet come to the surface of outer reality, might enable us to detect new archetypes rising in the horizon of consciousness and history. In the present case, we want to know if the archetype of duality has done its job, or if it will continue to rule our behavior, our thinking, and everything we do. In this case, there is little we can do. But I do not think this archetype still retains the monopolistic powers it had for the last two millennia.

Astrology assures us that the age of Aquarius is another story. One thing we can know for sure. The new archetype, the new star rising from the inner horizon in the sky of our minds has to do with the feminine principle. It is high time that we start to understand it. It does not mean that males will become effeminate. It does not mean that only females are its carriers. We are just beginning to understand that this is a cosmological principle that we all carry inside ourselves as a possibility of being human in a different way.

The new archetype will certainly create new social forms, new values, new ideas, and new minds. Can humanity chose an archetype and help it to manifest? This is a ticklish question. Jung was sure there was some kind of relationship between us and the archetypes, although he always said that they are, in themselves, unapproachable. If we are interested in them—that is, if consciousness takes a definite standpoint toward the unconscious—some interaction begins to take place. This is an interesting area, deserving much more attention than it has gotten so far. If a hundred people in a community would start working with their images, some new energy would be released and soon its effect might be perceptible. Our task now is to know what the feminine, the masculine, and the soul have to do with each other.

CHAPTER 3

Urban Trees
As Mirrors of the Soul

At this point I will bring in the feminine principle. We will again have more images than words.

Let me start by telling you how this research began. I am fortunate as a Jungian, because I feel free to research whatever I want to and plunge into all sorts of different adventures. With time, I have become aware that it is not my ego that actually decides what I have to do. It is something else that whispers, "Pay closer attention to that, go into it." I follow the "command" and am always rewarded, realizing how enriching those inner suggestions are, and how many more tools I have acquired to help us understand ourselves and the world we live in. This way of working has helped me to do something I profoundly trust, namely, bridging psychology and the world, psychology and the city, the landscape, art, politics, economics, culture.

After my training in Zurich I went back to Brazil in 1981 and opened a private practice. In 1985 I had the following experience: I was driving on one of our heavy traffic avenues. Looking to my right, I spotted a building being renewed. Seven small palm trees had been planted on the sidewalk for decoration purposes, and when I saw them I thought, "How nice, they are now planting palm trees." But I suddenly noticed a cluster of electrical wires just above them, and then I "heard" this phrase, "They will soon be decapitated." The next sentence was, "You must be a witness to what is happening." I wondered, "How can I be a witness?" "Photograph them," was the answer.

From that moment on, I realized that I had the task of taking pictures of threatened trees, collecting a certain number of images, and then trying to act as their mouthpiece to say whatever they would say if only they had a voice and could use words. It turns out that most of the trees I have so far photographed—more than one thousand now—are suffering trees. So my task has been to keep register not of beautiful trees about which you might say, "Look how gorgeous, all those flowers, look at the complex and elegant design the trunk, branches, and leaves make!" Mine is a collection of mutilated trees—trees that have been brutally attacked, planted in inadequate places, or prevented from following their own natural pattern of growth.

I had to understand this phenomenon and systematically find a way not just to say how awful or how sad this is. That would simply not be enough. A witness has to say more. So, I took this first photograph and then had to wait nine years until I was able to continue the work. I was not ripe, and the time was not right yet. Those nine years were like a pregnancy.

Nine years after this first photograph, I met the religious leader of an Afro-Brazilian religion called Umbanda, a mix between some elements of Catholicism and the ancient African cult of the Yoruba Orishas introduced by slaves in early colonial times. Umbanda is a typically Brazilian trance religion. A common friend arranged the meeting. I visited with this man in his country retreat, and we took a walk to talk while watching the trees. In the Yoruba pantheon there is a deity called Oshossi. He is the lord of the forest, the spirit of the trees, and he rules hunting. I asked this man, "What do you think Oshossi is feeling about the massive destruction of trees in the Amazon?" And this religious leader, who imperceptibly can fall into a trance, answered, "He is furious and wants his fury to come out, otherwise people will explode." Then I mentioned my experience with the palm trees and he said, "Oshossi commands you to do this work on his behalf."

That short conversation allowed me to make a psychological connection with an important synchronicity I had experienced some years before. As we know, synchronicities are not just interesting events to be talked about at leisure time. They have crucial roles in people's lives, because they catalyze energy and push their consciousness to expand. If people really connect to a synchronicity, something happens in their lives as a consequence. New energy starts to flow. A new goal appears to them.

I worked with Dr. Heinrich Karl Fierz, an outstanding analyst in Switzerland whom Jung had analyzed. He later became his close collaborator in the field of psychiatry, having been the co-founder, together with C. A. Maier, of the Zurichberg Clinic. It was mainly he who taught me how to be an analyst. He was like a Zen master, because he did not speak very much. Many times he would ask me a question, but, like with Zen koans, I did not know what the answer was or what he meant. He was always in contact with the unconscious dimension of reality and extremely connected to his deep intuitions. So it took me many, many years to understand the most precious lessons he wanted to teach me. When I returned to Brazil in 1981, I began a correspondence with him. He was growing extremely weak due to emphysema, and I had a growing depression. We exchanged letters, and he said a few things to me that I still have to work on. In 1984 he died. The synchronicity was imminent.

I had written what would become my last letter to him and was anxiously waiting for a reply. During the weekend I went away with my family and returned home on Sunday evening. Our first-floor apartment had glass walls in the lounge, through which we could be in close contact with a magnificent tree—many similar trees will be illustrated in the following pages. Its crown almost entered our room. My wife once followed for days in a row the routine of a bird building its nest until the chicks were ready to fly away. That tree was a wonderful companion. On that Sunday evening it was late. We put the children to bed. I felt strange and thought, "I don't know what it is, but something is wrong here."

Monday morning, when I came home for lunch, I looked out the window, and the tree was no longer there. It had been cut at the request of a police authority who lived across the street. The firefighters came and—for no apparent reason—cut down the tree. When I saw that empty space I was taken by a profound sadness, but I was not conscious yet of its long-term effect on me. When I came home again in the evening the porter approached me, "There is a letter for you." That was the only letter I did not have to open in order to know its contents. It was postmarked Zurich, and the envelope was black-rimmed, so I knew my dear friend had died. I then called his wife and realized that he had died at the exact moment the tree was cut down.

My dear analyst and the tree were gone together. I did not need a father figure any longer, and one of the tasks I had to fulfill was precisely to do this work with trees. Because I am a Jungian, I started with Jung, and went back once again to his unique paper called "The Philosophical Tree," in which he shows many images of trees drawn by patients.[1] In the opening of his paper he states that a tree is a mandala (magic circle in Sanskrit) seen from above. A mandala is a symbol of the Self. If you make a vertical section into a three-dimensional mandala you have a tree. In a tree you can visualize the deep structure of the psyche, an axis connecting above and below, both realms patterned in the same way, because roots and branches have exactly the same design. In the motive of the inverted tree, the roots look exactly like branches. Botanists determine how deep the roots reach by measuring the crown. Both have the same dimension up and down.

Jung often referred to the symbol of the tree as being ancient and similar in practically every culture and mythological system: the tree of life, the tree of knowledge, the tree of good and evil, of fertility, of ancestry. There are many myths about a tree sustaining the world, like Yggdrasil in Teutonic tradition, or about man's being born from a vagina in a tree trunk, or all the anthropomorphic and speaking trees in American Indian mythology.

Why is the tree such an eternal symbol? Because it is absolutely apt to convey all the complexities of the human psyche. Roots can be the topic for a whole discourse, as could the trunk, the branches, or the leaves, flowers, fruits, and seeds. Gaston Bachelard has written beautifully about most of these topics, drawing examples from literature and poetry.[2] We can reflect upon any of these aspects or consider synthetic statements, such as this strong one by the archetypal psychologist Thomas Moore, "Trees are our double in nature."[3] There is fraternity between them and us. They are our equivalent in the plant realm. There is a pre-verbal bond between us. Trees are much more our companions through life than animals, especially because they can survive us. A psychological connection with trees takes us directly into the realm of imagination. They are a perfect visualization of how imagination works: taking roots and branching out. So when a tree is cut, the link between consciousness and imagination, or between mind and spirit, is severed.

Remember Black Elk? He was the famous Sioux Indian, whose book made such a powerful impression on Jung, who often quoted it.[4] Black Elk knew that the Sioux were doomed, but he resisted as far as he could and enacted group rituals of which he had dreamed, in which the remaining of the tribe danced around the four points of the compass, with four different horses at each point. These rituals helped them to stay connected to the Self and fight back until one day he said something like, "The sacred tree is dead. There is no longer a center. We are finished when the sacred tree dies."

Originally, man was able to sense sacredness in trees. In all mythologies there are sacred trees. This feeling that there is a divine presence in a tree was essential to a whole way of being, and to a whole style of civilization. It is therefore a dangerous sign when that sense of sacredness that pervades nature, and trees in particular, is lost, whereupon they are treated either as timber, as something useful for us, or as landscape decoration. That loss of an awareness that tress are meaningful and valuable in and of themselves damages our spiritual connection and enhances our arrogance.

I am not just talking about preservation or ecology. We are different when we live in the company of trees. Their psychological impact on us is only beginning to be studied. It is difficult to put it into words, but people might feel a whole range of subtle things because of the presence of a tree. It might put them into contact with patience, perseverance, resistance, change through cycles, change and yet permanence, wisdom, tolerance, comfort, protection, poetry, beauty, transcendence. On a more scientific level, we also need trees because they help oxygenation, as well as the control of sound, wind, temperature, and luminosity. One single adult tree transpires four hundred liters of water per day, the same work done by five air conditioning machines.[5] They filter air and noise. They recycle the air we breathe. They soften the effects of heavy rain and wind. They shelter and nurture the fauna. They give us shade and repose.

Greater São Paulo has about ten million trees.[6] Ninety percent of them have been planted in inadequate places, under electrical wires, against walls, in the strip dividing traffic ways in air-polluted roads, in arid or somber lots. Their roots have to find their way through cement, gravel, rocks, and the thick net of underground telephone, power, gas, and water ducts. It was not a natural allocation of seeds carried by the wind or by birds that plotted them on the urban map but technical decisions as to the choice of specific trees in predetermined locations. Trees that naturally would grow to gigantic heights are planted under low electric high-tension cables. Somebody must have known beforehand that at some point in time the branches would touch the wires. Finally the power company workers declare the situation dangerous; it threatens power transmission. The decision to trim the branches as short as possible or to cut down the entire tree is quickly made, with the general approval of a passive population. Electrical wires always come first, and trees must be sacrificed at the slightest suspicion of danger. Thirty percent of all newly planted trees die after the first trimming. Seventy percent soon suffer physical attacks.

When you look at and read about the following illustrations, please try to listen to what all these trees would say if they could speak. Here is a first example of a kind of trimming supposedly done for the sake of safety, but which actually distorts the shape of the tree (see figure 16). To me this is like raping, so that electrical wires can freely run through it. Here we clearly see the polarity between nature and technology, tree and electric lamp post, which will appear repeatedly in this series. One year later, I went back to this same tree (see figure 17). First it was a young tree growing into a round shape, then central branches were cut, and one year later it was reduced to a crippled structure. Nobody cares, because with time the mass of new leaves will conceal the hurt part.

FIGURE 16

At a construction site for luxury apartment towers, contractors did not care for having a beautiful, mature tree in front of the future building. They cut all its branches at the trunk, provoking its death at the time when the building was ready. They even painted its dry trunk white, as a cement pillar, not to interfere with the cleanliness of the place.

One day, city workers came and pruned a tree in front of my office (see figure 18). I knew that in time it would die too. We can see the progressive loss of leaves a few months later (see figure 19) and the end result (see figure 20). When Christmas came, someone insensibly decorated a dead tree. From pre-Christian times, the Tree of Life was lit during the winter solstice to symbolize that life-giving light would return to the earth, as the tree itself would grow leaves again in spring. So it would be symbolically incoherent to light a dead tree. This one

FIGURE 17

was subsequently removed, and another one replaced it in the same inadequate location. It did not grow and died too.

Most of the trees in São Paulo are this kind (see figure 21). I love them, especially because the street where I was born and raised was lined—actually, the whole neighborhood, like others—with this kind of tree. It has blue flowers, and in springtime it is beautiful to see stretches of asphalt covered by a transient carpet of flowers. In this

FIGURE 18

FIGURE 19

FIGURE 20

picture we can see the complete, intact structure. Depending on how and to what degree a tree is pruned, it will never have its original structure again. What we have here is like a gothic cathedral, because full growth has not been curtailed. If that happens, there remains a caricature of the full potential of growth.

If we approach this fact symbolically, we can assess all its unseen consequences. A tree symbolizes our inner growth, and ideally this should not be trimmed, nor mutilated, nor stopped in any way. We will

Urban Trees as Mirrors of the Soul (67)

FIGURE 21

now develop this idea of the mirror effect of mutilated trees, which in a gigantic underdeveloped metropolis symbolize and reflect curtailed psychological processes. Economists would say underdevelopment, and I would say mutilated development—reflected outside in suffering trees that mirror our unconscious situation.

Common mentality wrongly assumes that it is good to trim trees once in a while, similar to having our hair cut. New hair will grow with renewed strength. However, the analogy is false. Trees in nature do not need to be pruned to be strong. No one is there to provide that service. So where did we get the idea that trees should have their branches cut? Why do people feel relieved and at peace with their consciousness when that happens? "When spring comes, new leaves will sprout. It is all right; it is good for the tree."

I studied botany a bit to understand what happens when a branch is severed.[7] The first organic reaction is for the immune system to close up the wound as soon as possible, so that bacteria will not invade. It is a natural defense reaction against a foreign body. The immune system of the tree, after a limb is severed, creates a ring-shaped scar. The wound closes, but the principle regulating growth gets disorganized. At the traumatic spot, an excessive number of new, thin branches quickly appears (see figure 22), as if the tree were desperately trying to compensate for the loss of that one branch by creating a hundred new ones in its place. It is a crazy multiplication of cells at excessive speed—an impossible situation. These new branches do not survive after a few weeks. There is obviously not room for one hundred branches. I was moved to realize that the tree wants to stay alive, that it does all it can to generate new cells, but that it all happens in a chaotic way. The Self was hurt so badly that it can no longer organize the whole being. The attacked and traumatized tree has lost its wisdom, and its desperate attempt at restoring life will inevitably fail.

Some time ago, the power company sent a pamphlet to all citizens who pay monthly power bills, urging customers to call them about any trees close to electrical posts—the company would be glad to come and cut them. I noticed that the post in the illustration resembled a cross, as if the power company were unconsciously saying that actually they intended to crucify trees. Again, like in the previous chapter, I had to

FIGURE 22

deal with the crucifixion motif, but this is so ironic because the cross is itself a tree. There are images of Christ crucified on a tree, and the cross is made of a trunk. So here, one tree would be crucified on the other. This is certainly food for archetypal thinking. The sacrifice of nature in the cross. Again, why must nature carry the cross for us? Is nature sinful? Nature does not need resurrection. We do.

Some years ago, in a small town in the country, city planners decided to plant only a certain kind of medium-size tree. It looks like a bouquet, and its flowers look like orchids. Perhaps due to ideological contamination from the capital, they also began to trim these short trees. A few beans with seeds were left alone. Seeds will fall on asphalt. Many country towns like this one are experiencing quick economic development, but this process is one-sided, in the sense that values remain underdeveloped. The awareness is still thin that technology, as in the sorcerer's apprentice story, can turn against its creator.

I found two drastic examples of mutilation in middle-class, downtown São Paulo neighborhoods. In the first case, despite the absence of overhanging electrical wires, workers cut the branches of a tree. The end result sadly reminded me of severed fingers in a hand. This attack on the tree goes beyond the conflict between nature and technology. In the other example (see figure 23), we have a tree that, after being deprived of its structural balance, looks like a disoriented living being that no longer knows where its axis stands.

Now we have to address projection, as we did in the second chapter. We certainly project something onto trees, something we have great difficulty acknowledging in ourselves, and that is our dark, dangerous side. We also project on them our growth complex—present in most Third World societies—the historical incapacity to connect the ancestral roots of our psyche to a difficult, complex colonial process that did to our identity something similar to what we see in these suffering trees.

FIGURE 23

The question of growth has to be treated in a differentiated way. The First World has now to deal with limits, as the mythology of unlimited growth has revealed its destructive dimension in all aspects of modern life. But for other regions the problem is of another kind, because growth has gone wrong. Before it is limited, it has to be redirected along new guidelines and values. As there is a collective unconscious complex affecting this whole area, we tend to avoid the responsibility of facing the drastic changes involved in redefining the kind of growth we should have. There is something of adolescent psychology here: the fear of looking at oneself in the mirror and seeing who one really is, what one is doing to oneself. Trees are this mirror. We are in conflict with our need to grow. Then we attack the growth of trees.

When I reached this understanding, I went to a specialist to talk about the House-Tree-Person test. In the test, developed in the early 1950s, a person is asked to draw a tree. A manual is used to help interpretation, but it tends to become too technical. There are many details that can be measured. Something intriguing at a certain point in the trunk can be correlated to a certain age, when presumably a significant event took place in that person's life. Many people are experts at doing that. The idea then came to me that all the pictures I had taken were like a tree test unconsciously done by the population at large. City dwellers draw their collective tree test on living trees. No more drawings are necessary for us to understand the situation. It is all there for us to see.

Next is a picture from a test done by a ten-year-old boy, Rodrigo (see figure 24). Notice the little branches. After a trauma, a tree gets disorganized, and it shoots out an excessive number of new branches in an attempt to preserve life and growth, but they are destined to die. Rodrigo's father left home when he was still a baby. Until his third year he lived with his grandmother. During this period and later he had constant panic attacks, in which he feared he would lose his mother. At ten he was unable to attend school regularly because of his deep-seated insecurity. His father had completely abandoned him and started a new family. The tree he drew depicts his inner situation. He has lost father and is insecure of losing mother too. He is desperately trying to recover his process of psychological growth, but that will fail, as it does

FIGURE 24

when actual trees suffer a severe trauma (see figure 25). If we refer to the ideas exposed in the previous chapter, we can try to interpret this actual tree test and say on its behalf, "My community has lost the father principle and is terribly afraid of losing mother, so it gets disorganized and no longer knows in which direction it has to grow." The first tree belongs to Rodrigo alone, but a similar one on the sidewalk belongs to eighteen million people and has something to say about all of them.

Daniela is a thirteen-year-old girl. She went into therapy because at school she was apathetic, almost catatonic, so closed-in that her teacher thought she was an autistic child, which in fact she was not.

FIGURE 25

She oversleeps, is absolutely careless, and clings to stronger girls for guidance and as models of feminine identity. Her self-esteem is dangerously low. Her tree has no leaves, except for one at the upper right corner, which soon will fall as the others did. This is the image of death in life, catatonia, apathy. This same tree can be seen out in the streets, yet not necessarily in autumn. Leaves fall because the tree is dead in life.

Rafael is a twelve-year-old boy. He was often spanked and humiliated by his parents when he was a young child. At one point, his father got so jealous of his mother that after one of their frequent violent fights he went into the garage, started the engine and killed himself breathing carbon monoxide. The boy was away on a trip. When he returned home he was told about his father's terrible death. He fell into a shock state, was soon taken to a child therapist, and drew his tree. It is full of aggressive shapes like saws and knives. Absolutely brown, it has no trace of green. No roots to be seen, and no leaves at all. The trauma Rafael suffered turned him into a destructive and anti-social boy. He wants to kill too, as his father did.

Now compare his drawing with a butchered magnolia tree. I have for years admired the beauty of its unique white, hard flowers. Magnolias were originally brought to the city by Italian immigrants, as a remembrance of their beloved landscape. The senseless and violent attack it suffered can only be understood if we search for an unconscious, old trauma in the collective psyche that forces it to act out the same destructiveness that has befallen it in some forgotten time.

Let us move to another topic: the base of trees and the space surrounding them. I do not know if this happens elsewhere, but in São Paulo people consider this particular spot the ideal place to dump garbage and all kinds of undesirable materials. In ancient times, the place where certain trees emerged from the ground was considered sacred. In India, for instance, at the base of holy trees the Hindus make altars for Shiva, consisting of an iron trident, garlands of flowers, a stone lingam, a saffron colored stone, and votive lamps, all ritually assembled. Why would an archetypally sacred place decay to the state of garbage deposit? Does this arrangement not speak eloquently about our loss of sacredness?

This psychological attitude is so widespread that it can be detected beyond city limits, reaching the rural area. For example, a tree in the middle of a sugar-cane field was cut for apparently no other reason except to mark, like a gravestone, a garbage dumping site. When we look at the city or at landscapes with the kind of approach we are developing here, we instantly understand what may be happening to people. A contact is established with a deep layer of the collective psyche, allowing us to assess urban problems from a new angle. Ignorance and unconsciousness as destructive projections are at the root of the greatest part of these complex problems. Consider, for instance, a plastic garbage bag hanging from the frail branch of a meager, weak tree. Such an image expresses our contempt for living trees.

Latin America's most advanced hospital, called Albert Einstein, was built by the Jewish community in São Paulo. The compound is always being remodeled and expanded. Amidst the constant activity, a bare trunk in the parking lot captured my attention. A forgotten tree seems not to deserve any special attention, and that says something about the shadow of institutional health care, which tends to overlook individual needs.

It is beyond my reach to understand why anybody would cut down a palm tree at a beach, but I found an unfortunate example of this at an oceanside resort. The tree must have been the recipient of a negative projection. Dead trees, reduced to stumps, are perhaps the saddest outer images of the devastating effects of arrested inner growth.

Did you know that we have an inverted tree in our chest? The circulatory system in our lungs branches out according to a tree structure. Therefore trees are not only symbolic. If these trees are pruned by disease, breathing is affected, and life is at risk.

Similarly, we can contrast an actual tree to the structure of the coronary artery, with all its branches and ramifications. Of course, each small blood vessel has a fundamental life function and cannot be trimmed randomly. In a heart attack, part of this tree dies; physical death might occur. As I maintain that trees are maltreated as a result of our projections upon them, the parallel here is crucial. If the heart becomes the recipient of projected shadow and not of our highest values and feelings, that psychological, unconscious phenomenon can trigger a whole chain of somatic malfunctions, from high blood pressure to dysrhythmia, blockages, thrombosis, and insufficient circulation of blood and psychic energy. Images no longer circulate through the cardiac tree; its vital imaginal sap solidifies. We are unfortunately still unconscious of this central mystery about the free flow of images in our psyche. We ignore that we breathe images. We eat them, and we poison or heal ourselves with them.

Not only blood vessels but also the liver, nerves in the brain, and muscles in the face, hands, and feet are organized according to a tree pattern. We realize then that this structure appears in all forms of life, both physical and spiritual. Cells assemble and grow like trees. Memory and knowledge unfold as trees, through roots, trunks, branches, and smaller branches. The old myth of the tree of knowledge is an apt representation of a mental process that nowadays can be clearly described by evolutionary neurobiology.

On a larger scale, this same tree structure exists in the delta of a river. When a river finally reaches the sea, it branches out like a gigantic tree. The whole earth, like a body, displays a variety of tree images when looked at from a satellite. In that aerial view appear tree tests done by nature, and in that case the tree is never mutilated—except when there is human interference.

Children have a wise habit of giving images to their parents or other persons they love. Gifts of this sort must be viewed with utmost respect and attention, because they may express deep contents of a child's soul, or the way the soul sees things. When I was eight I dedicated a small drawing to my father, which reappeared in one of his wallets some years after his death (see figure 26). In it there is a house, a pathway, trees, the two fishes I mentioned in the first chapter, and—to my

FIGURE 26

amazement because I have become a Jungian analyst—two chairs facing each other and a vase with two flowers between them. I hesitated to include this picture and a few others that will follow, fearing that they were too personal, but that is not at all the point. I believe this material can show clearly the importance of drawing as a way to open channels for the emergence of unconscious contents that in the course of time may become of central importance in a person's life. If those drawings, paintings, or other expressive objects somehow reappear in a later moment, one realizes that the individuation process is not arbitrary and really consists in gradually becoming what one already is at the beginning, exactly like a tree.

Children have that gift of spontaneous expression, but almost all will lose it sooner or later. In my case, when I entered college I left the art school and concentrated all my energies in following two faculties, law and social sciences, which demanded all available time. I clearly remember that I increasingly felt uneasy about drawing. Self-criticism reached a point at which nothing was good enough to deserve attention. The mind, then, gained primacy over all other aspects of psychic life. Only many years later, when I began my analytical training in Zurich, did I consider taking drawing and painting back again and, as it happened, in a very modest way—not with special papers and pencils but in a small notebook that I also used to write down dreams. Please overlook the personal side of the story. I use it to show how, when we make room for it, a creative process starts unfolding under the conscious surface, aiming at goals of which we have no hints.

My first "official" drawing of this period is a simple sketch of a weed sprouting from a crack in the cement (see figure 27). The weed had caught my attention during one of my frequent walks in Zurich. It took me years to realize that my drawing was both a self-portrait and the first manifestation of this whole reflection. I was doing this and other drawings at a time when I had absolutely no idea that one day I would lecture about trees. Nevertheless, the unconscious seemed to have known it much before, paving the way, arranging synchronicities, making me responsive and sensitive to a problem that had been overlooked by collective consciousness. I can see now that indications came through these unpretentious drawings. At a later moment, a meaning-

FIGURE 27

ful connection is made, and then we know that the major concerns of our life were already present as anticipations in our soul much before any awareness was possible. Such is the link between these two realms.

Next is a drawing depicting a strange dream image that I had at that time (see figure 28). In analysis, I heard that "something new wants to grow from an old, rigid structure." Twelve years later I was trying to understand this image, the conflict between trees and electric posts. My old dream image encourages me to believe that the problem has to be worked on at a deep psychic level, until iron sprouts—which could only mean new openings in consciousness to perceive heretofore ignored aspects of life. It is not technology versus nature, but the two merging into a third entity, which is actually the dream of all ecologically minded people who work on this modern alchemical process.

Indians in Brazil paint soul visions and perceptions of reality that sharply contrast with our current views. We have not yet been able to part with our arrogance and start to learn from their images something we badly need to understand—what technology, civilization, and our mythology of unlimited growth have being doing to life on earth. A Ticuna Indian from the Amazon region painted an image showing the spirit that inhabits a certain tree. In the painting, a shaman heals a

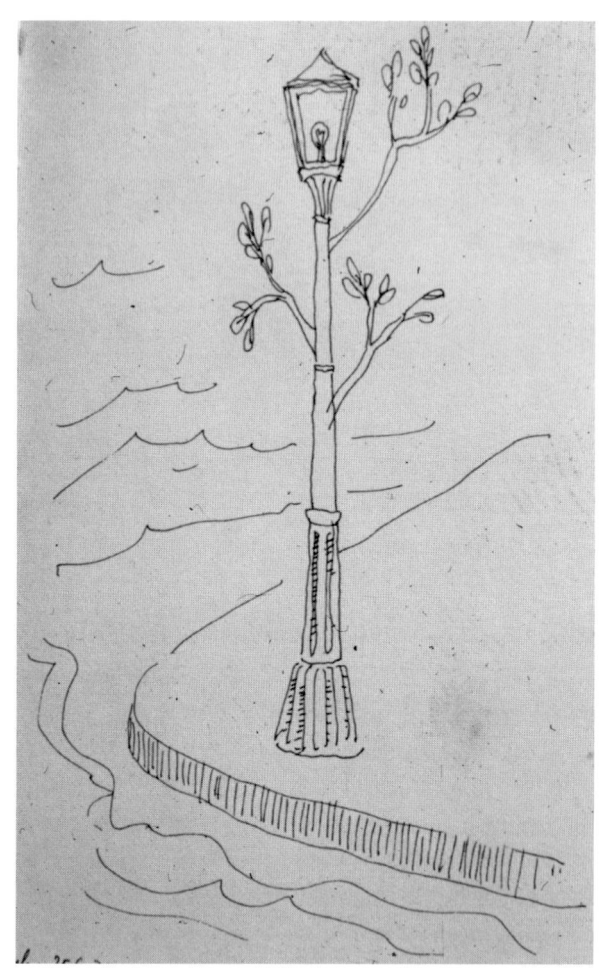

FIGURE 28

person's wounds with the intermediation of the tree spirit. The message is clear: the medicine man is only a medium for the workings of the transcendental dimension. In Indian culture, people recognize and respect this connection. They know that if a tree is attacked the spirit goes away. They know man is too weak and too small to endure suffering alone.

Another tribe, the Kamayurá of Central Brazil, performs a yearly ritual to honor its ancestors called Quarup, in which the spirit of the deceased is represented by a trunk covered with paintings. These trunks are cut a long distance away and brought to the central square, where they stay erect for the whole duration of the ritual. In their belief, the creator god made humanity by sculpting human forms on tree trunks; therefore, those who died since the last celebration are represented in their essential form. This is another kind of meaningful connection established by culture, religion, and mythology between humanity, trees, and creation. That is why Indians have, for thousands of years, preserved the forest for us, one could say. But now that we have power to rule over lands that were once only theirs and means to dissolve the inner strength of their ancient beliefs, we reduce trees to timber, to objects of commercial exchange, and lure the Indians to cut the trees down for low prices. This is the apex civilization has reached. It has succeeded in changing the traditional attitude the Indian people had toward nature, making them do the dirty work for beads.

For city dwellers, tree trunks have lost all the symbolic meaning they had in the past and are seen just as a potential danger, as is stressed by newspapers whenever trees fall after a tempest. What is not mentioned, however, is that roots have no space to penetrate, because the urban underground upon which they are planted is occupied by a web of electrical and telephone cables, gas, water, and sewage ducts. It is easier to project the treacherous quality of potential danger on trees than to work honestly on the irrationality of urban anti-life equipments.

But there is still hope, if at least a few people contact with trees. Somebody materialized their suffering by painting on a stump eyes that cry tears of blood (see figure 29). Not only is the tree crying, it is also looking directly to us, hoping perhaps to awaken in us an awareness badly needed for us to overcome the dangerous—*this* danger is not a projection—one-sidedness into which we have blindly fallen.

Because I have been referring to Indians and their cultural attitudes toward nature and trees, I have chosen to close these observations with an image that portrays a central scene in the Indian myth of the tree-boy. He was born and has roots for feet, leaves for hair, and is mothered by the jaguar. Indians believe that our tree dimension, that part of us that is able to feel brotherhood with all living beings, has to be nurtured not by the intellectual mother but by that instinctive intelligence that

FIGURE 29

knows that body, coronary system, psychology, imagination, and spirit must merge and grow together as a whole being.

 We Jungians are also part of a tree that begins with Jung as a trunk but that has deep roots in the great explorers of the soul from all times. Jung's followers, like branches, carry on his pursuits. We all can find a place in this flowering creation of our modern culture.

CHAPTER 4

The Alchemy of Cement in a Modern City

We are all familiar with the terrible urban problems that affect our modern cities. Traditionally, we have handed these problems over to city planners, engineers, politicians, people working with public finances, or social workers. We are unaccustomed to thinking that urban problems are a mirror of our own inner condition.

I live in the third-largest city in the world, São Paulo, which has eighteen million inhabitants. The second-largest city is Bombay, in India. São Paulo is very close in size to Mexico City. The head of this problematic list is Tokyo, with almost twenty-eight million people living together. In cities this large, there are people who never see the sunrise, people who do not get light in their apartments, and people who can never look at the stars. Their children, who probably have never seen a chicken or a cow, will become afraid to go out in the streets and to participate openly in the community, because people do not know each other anymore. Violence keeps growing. There is lack of beauty. There is lack of poetry, and there is a sad lack of soul. Big cities are made of cement. So cement is the matter, the *prima materia* with which cities are built.

Alchemy is an ancient way of looking at reality and its possible ways of transformation. According to alchemy, a metamorphosis occurs when you have two poles, or two different principles, combined in the same vessel. The hermetic vessel is sealed, and transformation starts to develop by its own accord. The alchemist does not interfere; he only prays and keeps a low fire. He prays that God brings about a transformation.

In this chapter I will contend that a city has its own unconscious that can be examined through a series of urban art works. I will deal with the unconscious of eighteen million people and explore it on a deep level—something they ignore.

When a patient comes into therapy, the therapist listens to a conscious story, which will be told by means of quite commonplace phrases and images. The patient communicates his or her pain as best as possible. Having gone through that initial narrative, both therapist and patient will search for signals or images that might be rooted in that person's unconscious, because the main idea is that this profound, unknown dimension of the psyche hypothetically will be working out a way to heal the wounds, disharmonies, or wrong attitudes that are troubling this particular individual.

We are aware that it is not the therapist that heals, through his or her wise words and interpretations. The analyst—as an intermediate figure—puts the patient in contact with his or her own inner healing forces. When the patient goes through that process, serious, gradual, and profound transformations take place inside that person.

I look at the city in the same way. The city is suffering. Why? Because it has lost its soul. Is the city going to a therapist? No, there is no such person as a city therapist. There are city planners; there are urban committees. Yet we have not reached a point where we would assemble a group of specialists to take care of the wounds affecting the soul of the city. We still do not know how to talk or think in those terms. But we could certainly attempt to do this. We could put together a historian, an artist, a teacher, a physician, an analyst, a philosopher, a musician, an ecologist, together with an engineer, a politician, and a former comedian, and start talking about the problem. But maybe the time is not right for it yet. The question then arises: who is trying to express what the city itself might be feeling and going through? Mainly the artists. There is a kind of artist who is not so much impressed with the professional persona, such as being a success, reaching high prices for the work done, and making a lot of money, but who really is a medium, an intermediary between the unconsciousness of the city and our common consciousness. This kind of artist creates a kind of deep well that establishes a connection between those underground waters and the surface level of our common perception of things as they appear to us. He or she facilitates an alchemical process.

Artists, establishing that connection, can bring up symbols or images that—if we are willing to do so—we can absorb and integrate on a collective mental level. They do their work and we, the citizens, can attempt to understand the contents they are bringing up, perhaps translating them into scientific, technical, or educational language, infusing the old, habitual consciousness with new ideas and values. Only when collective consciousness starts to change can we expect significant transformations in our cities. We can then realize that urban problems are not just for engineers; they are first and foremost psychic problems. Hence, there is a need for analysts to be involved in healing the troubled collective psyches of our cities.

For some aspects of reality, artists are the best conveyors of what is happening in subtle dimensions. They can contact what is still hidden. They can make positive and negative prognoses. For other things artists are quite inept. But for some complicated human problems, we have to go to the artist. The artist's social role is not simply to provide people with aesthetically meaningful objects, but to be a psychopomp, a guide into unknown territory. In my view, this is the function of art in a community. This is the healing role art can play, not just the promotion of what fits inner decoration, but the revelation of something hidden or unconscious that even a good Jungian analyst would be unable to detect.

In the previous chapter, I presented trees as a test completed by the population as a whole. In this chapter I want to go a bit deeper and show that every city has a discourse of its own: something specific to say about itself, about its prognosis, and about what should be worked out and dealt with at a very deep level. As I mentioned before how my tree reflection began, I will also tell you how this piece of work came into being.

In the late nineties, a group of artists, architects, photographers, musicians, historians, and philosophers got together and decided to start a yearly exhibit of art—not in museums, not in art galleries, but in significant places of the city. The first exhibit was held in an old, downtown São Paulo building that was being used for minor public services. It was an extremely neglected and ugly looking spot. In that building, for the first time, an art exhibit was presented, and it was about the city itself. A second one was held the following year in a nineteenth-century slaughterhouse, and then there was a third one in 1997, which is the one I will discuss.

To go to this exhibit, patrons started in the old central train station, a beautiful, red brick structure planned and erected by an English company. That elegant train station was once a symbol of progress and urbanization and was widely used by the upper classes, but nowadays only poor people use the railroad to go back and forth from home to work. Exhibit-goers would start in this train station, take a special train, ride for some ten minutes, and then exit in the unexpected place where the exhibit began.

After I arrived there with my wife, I felt my bowels moving in a way they sometimes strangely do. I knew that something wanted to come up to my conscious mind; I knew that non-verbal emotion was trying to be transformed into insights and meanings. So it suddenly dawned on me that perhaps I could look at this art exhibit as a sequence of alchemical works. When that was clear, I went back to my scientific training, and I said: "OK, I had an insight. I have a hypothesis and must test it. If not, I am just having my own trip." Of course, I had to contemplate a few works to check if the whole idea made sense. To my surprise, it made sense throughout the exhibit until the last piece. We then went back home. I took some notes and then decided that I would let this experience unfold inside me. I knew neither the artists' names nor the titles they had given their pieces. Interviewing them seemed unnecessary, and talking to others was not what would inspire me. I believed that I had to let the symbolic meaning of each piece start to talk to me.

I will now return to that exhibit and visit it again while I share my impressions. It may not make sense to you, because some of you certainly live in pleasant and healthy places; however, I believe that you know cities like Houston, Chicago, Detroit, Cleveland, Boston, or New York, places I have been. There are so many American cities with the same kinds of problems as the ones we will talk about.

In Dallas, Texas, there is an institute, originally founded by James Hillman, carrying on this kind of work.[1] Some very good people there talk about the soul of the city, the "anorexia nervosa" of slim buildings, the "paranoia" of fenced-in houses, the psychological meaning of walking. They talk about the symbolic meaning of roofs, windows, walking, white lighting, shades, carpets. I love that. They are certainly opening up new ground, bridging interior decoration and archetypal psychology or industrial design and the psyche. I think that is all exciting. I do not officially belong to that group. I do not consider myself an archetypal psychologist, nor am I a follower of that school of thought. But I think it is a good thing that similar ideas spring up in different places and in different people. Without any institutional connections, we are doing something along parallel lines. But, as I said before, I just want to follow what my soul wants me to do.

Let us now start with the illustrations and images. The first one is an aerial view of downtown São Paulo (see figure 30), in which you can see two railways that form an island, because you cannot reach that area by foot or by car—it is completely closed in. Right in the middle is the place where the exhibit was held. One building was a flour mill, built around 1940 along the railway tracks so that the heavy sacks full of white flour could be directly transported to the seaport in Santos. In the 1960s, the firm went bankrupt, and the mill was abandoned. Soon it turned into a modern ruin. This is the place we are going to enter.

Looking closer, it is reminiscent of bombarded buildings during wartime. This is right in the heart of São Paulo. If it were not for the exhibit, I would have never been to this place, because it is located in an urban island that is like a forbidden garden. But what kind of a garden is this? It is clearly not the Garden of Paradise, not the Garden of Aphrodite or the Virgin Mary, not the garden of the Troubadours. It is the Garden of the Shadow. Being a secluded area in the city, this is where

FIGURE 30. Aerial view of exhibit site.

dealers trade forbidden drugs, thieves hide stolen valuables, and where hoodlums spend the night. In the heart of a metropolis there is a secret garden where the shadow thrives. This is where the artists gathered, as in a black ritual, to invoke the unconscious to manifest.

Our scene is not in a white marble museum, nor in an art school, but in this fetid, repulsive place, inside a decaying, ruined building.

Windowpanes have disappeared. The place looks ghostly. It was full of debris before the artists moved in (see figure 31), and they chose to create their work right on the spot. Nothing was brought ready to be installed. The first things the artists saw were weeds, broken walls, dust, water infiltration, rats, cockroaches, dirt, and shit. Soul must be created—rekindled—out of the *nigredo*.

In the exhibit's first work, artists covered part of the building with a red plastic veil (Carlos Nader, *Red Veil*). In alchemy, you have three basic colors: black, white, and red. Black is called *nigredo*, the darkest dark, corresponding to the first stage of the *prima materia* once it starts to undergo a process of change. Some authors have called it the night sea journey, the dark night of the soul, the black sun, depression, and melancholia. After black comes white, *albedo*, and then red, *rubedo*. In veiling this dead body with red, the artist is bringing blood back to what has died. The infusion of blood renews a psychic circulation of images.

In the second work, a silo was cut at its base (Ricardo Ribenboim, *Silo*). There remained six large iron vessels, three of which were filled with dirty water. In the first was the skeleton of a cow. The middle contained a small, motorized pump underwater releasing air bubbles to the dark surface. And in the third, some charcoal pieces floated around. When I looked at this scene I was sure that an authentically alchemical

FIGURE 31. The abandoned mill before the exhibit.

The Alchemy of Cement in a Modern City

procedure was taking place, because work was being done with dead water. Dead water is what runs in our polluted rivers. There are no longer any fishes. No one can row a boat or sit by the river bank because its water stinks; it is lethally polluted and contaminated by deadly bacteria. An unconscious voice seems to be saying: "Let's work with dead water, let's pump some air back into it." Air is spirit, breath of life, purification, and oxygenation of what has gone putrid. Charcoal also purifies water. So the first symbolic statement is that the primal waters of life have to be purified. Psychic waters have been polluted, imagination darkened, movement lost, and light nearly out, but that can be worked upon through alchemical imagination itself. Only when this understanding is reached can the water pollution problem be solved by technical means and not the reverse.

The following work, called *Dwelling* by Rodrigo Andrade, consisted just of a pile of railway ties. It was as if the artist had said: "Let the railroad be rolled back in upon itself. Let us recoil, regress, go back inward. Let not the tracks expand out into open country, but back toward their own center. Let them re-flect." So let us reflect on what a dwelling is. We live in a city that has a large proportion of dwellings that do not deserve that name, for they do not protect their inhabitants. They do not shelter them and thereby do not provide adequate inner space for the soul. Many of us have houses, but are they dwellings? Only in alchemy will you find a house that houses no one. It is a paradoxical dwelling place, as if to say, we need to create inner space before we continue to build endlessly outward. Inner space has been occupied by decaying matter instead of by the spirit. So this is the way we are living. I do not think that an architect, an engineer, or a technician could speak about our present-day condition better than this artist did with his paradoxical dwelling place.

The next work was titled *House of Lanterns*, created by Marcelo Dantas and Roberto Moreira. It was completely blacked out, and we needed flashlights to visit it. Contrary to *Dwelling,* in which we contacted the disappearance of inner space, here we tried to find our way wandering through absolutely empty space. In previous times, when the mill was still active, laborers worked with wheat to transform it into white, pure flour. Now the place is completely abandoned, full of debris, garbage, excrement, waste paper, rags, and dripping water. What did the artist feel here? He blackened the place, and then he installed electric sensors on the ceiling. As we walked in and around, strategically placed sensors activated audio tapes. We heard sounds of police sirens, gunshots, enraged dogs barking, swarming bees, and anxious babies crying. You must imagine yourself walking into this place, in total darkness except for a flashlight, listening to those sounds. Where are you? What is that? You are in Hades. That is the Palace of Death and Darkness. What this means is that if we want to undergo a process of transformation, we have to descend first to the realm of the archetypal shadow. We have to go to Hades and understand what the shadow is autonomously doing through all these horrible urban problems it creates, which must be grasped in the first place as outer reflections of our collective inner Hades. We have to go there and get our hands dirty with soot, mud, and shit in order to start this work without gloves. We must acknowledge the degree to which we are all responsible for poverty, misery, social injustice, criminality, juvenile delinquency, epidemics, malnutrition, famine, and all the rest of it.

Dante started his journey descending into Hell in the company of Virgil. There would be no Divine Comedy without Dante's journey into the underground of human immorality. And this is what the artist tells the visitor: "You must go there if you want to see what comes out of it." Then we could proceed to the next place.

We then walked upon solid concrete floor (see figure 32). The artist had dozens of tiny holes drilled in it along crossed orthogonal lines, forming a grid, and then in each hole he inserted a plastic, disposable syringe filled with liquid mercury. In the middle he placed a huge crack pipe. Before we approached it, it looked like a miniature army of aligned marching soldiers, or a group of students performing rhythmic gymnastics. The monitor who was accompanying us delivered comments and explanations based exclusively on a common-sense, conscious point of view, and at this point she said: "Here the artist is working with the drug addiction problem." That was too obvious. All big cities have a drug problem, and you make poor art if you just assemble syringes and a crack pipe. But when I looked at that, the Roman god Mercury instantly came to my mind. Alchemy worked with three main

FIGURE 32. Cildo Meirelles, *Crack Pipe and Syringes*

elements: salt, sulfur, and mercury. Mercury is a precipitator of change. Salt and sulfur react violently to it. Which unconscious image is the artist bringing to the surface here? It is the symbol of the injection of mercury into cement. Through his art, he seems to say: "If you really want to deal with the drug problem, you have to bring soul back to cement. You must try this injection of subtle substances to make it react through the alchemical action of mercury."

What does that mean, bringing soul back to cement? This is a metaphor. Actually, it means bringing soul back to our hardened and rigid psyches, we citizens, to make us sensitive to what cement stands for and to what excessive cement causes in ourselves. We must therefore be infused with the spirit of mercury. Jung wrote an essay, "The Spirit Mercurius," which has to do with the workings of the transcendent function in ourselves, an instinctual capacity we possess to symbolize ways of overcoming insoluble situations for which we see no conscious way out.[2] Therefore, it is possible to give up naive projections according to which the drug problem should exclusively be dealt with by health or police authorities. As this is first and foremost a psychological problem, the injection of mercury will unleash new values and ideas, which subsequently can be delegated to technicians and city planners to implement them as public policies.

In the next piece, the artist used the language of photography engraved on copper plates, a modern version of the old daguerreotypes in the early stages of this art (Patrícia Azevedo, *Photos on Copper Plates*). Her work superimposed photographs taken from the same angle, some in 1914, others in 1940, and the rest in the present, 1997. She made double exposures of similar negatives from different time periods and then transferred the resulting synchronous images to large copper plates that she hung on the wall as imaginal windows. The plates were corroded by acid, blurring some details of the pictured scenes. A viewer's first reaction might be: "I get it, the artist is talking about the passing of time. She is telling me this was a nice working place in the past, and now it is reduced to shambles. Time does actually corrode all we build. Everything in the end disappears."

This is a normal reading of the work, but it is just too conscious—we do not need art to remember that. Art, after all, can change us: it can go deeper. If you want to make a reading that catches the unconscious contents, you have to go back to copper and corrosion. Copper is the metal of Aphrodite. The images that appear in Aphrodite's mirror when she looks at herself, or in the reddish reflections of copper, have to do with love. Loving the image. Corrosion is the defacement of the image. Is it a good or a bad thing that images get corroded? It depends on which images we are considering. If a city has its memory corroded, the old trees, the squares in front of the church, the humble row of houses, the river bank, the horse fountain, the old jail, the first bank, the factories built by immigrants—to lose all that has negative consequences for our sensibility and sense of identity. That is bad. Outer icons of collective memory die, threatening the inner building of memory. People will forget from where they have come. But there is a

The Alchemy of Cement in a Modern City (93)

kind of image that definitely has to be corroded in order to make room for new configurations.

We have a mental and photographic image of which we are still proud: São Paulo was once the fastest-growing city in the world. That was in the fifties. The period's economic statistics, the number of new houses being built per day, and the tons and tons of concrete used illustrate the extremely accelerated rate of growth São Paulo experienced then. We are used to thinking that we could be number one in the world. "We grow so fast that we will soon catch up with the First World, and that is wonderful." I believe that that image has to be corroded. The new phrase, with an accompanying image is "Stop growing." As Luigi Zoja has convincingly demonstrated in his excellent book, *Growth and Guilt*, modern civilization has reached the zenith of hubris in its belief that unlimited growth would be the ultimate achievement of humanity.[3] The tragic results of this age-long presumption is exploding everywhere around us, from the ozone hole to the contamination of underground water and from mania to depression as collective syndromes.

Inspired by art, we must go back in time and superimpose our modern ways with old ways for the sake of enlightenment. Are there not a few vital things that we regret having lost? Think of Sunday morning peacefulness, shopping in the old central market, talking to a neighbor, sitting in a downtown park, and taking a rest near a clear stream. There is a problem, art is saying, with images. They must be reflected in all their clarity in Aphrodite's copper mirror. She must like what she is shown. She will definitely not negotiate.

Continuing through the art exhibit, we encountered a place where we could look at the floor above, because three big squares had been cut out (Nelson Félix, *Cut Squares on the Floor*). They hung in mid-air, suspended by iron cables, like heavy, flat pendulums in slow motion. People may have all sorts of different reactions to this scene, and mine was that alchemical forces are saying: "You must now create breaks and put separations down. You have to open channels of communication between above and below. Cut, pierce, and displace cement, so you may have a new perspective."

No longer boxed in, we can become conscious of other dimensions: one above and the other below. Most of us who live in apartments actually are confined in cement boxes. We forget it, but in reality we are separated—by slim walls—from other destinies enacted just a few meters away, at left and right. Above your head or below your feet a baby is being conceived. A couple is divorcing; a child is drawing a picture; someone is sighing; a burglar is stealing; a despairing soul wants to die. The human drama unfolds all around, but we are boxed in our little cubes—not cardboard shoe boxes but hard cement ones, all decorated inside. We delude ourselves thinking that by merely looking out our windows we are in communication. That is just visual contact. What is lacking is psychic communication. Or, one step further, communication between the conscious mind and the unconscious. As we are all split, these two levels are concretely separated by a thick cement floor. The unconscious psyche told the artist, who passes the word on to us by cutting open the barrier that separates us from the unconscious above and below.

There is no sensuality in the works we have been discussing, as there is no sensuality in the big city. The city is harsh. It has pointed angles that wound us. It is hard—we knock ourselves against it. The city is not sensuous. It does not caress us and does not invite us to caress it. It does not embrace us. It does not laugh with us. We cannot touch our faces to a wall—it will hurt. We no longer have much wood in the city. We have hardly any soft materials. We have steel, concrete, plastic, black rubber, asphalt, and all kinds of hard surfaces.

The next work was done by a woman who, instead of cutting squares, pierced a small hole through the cement floor, upon which she assembled a pile of sand (see figure 33). The exhibit lasted forty-five days, and that was the span of time it took for all this sand to run down through the tiny hole to the floor below. In the upper floor, only a pile of sand was visible, but when viewers came to the lower floor, or vice versa, they realized what was happening. The first, automatic association is with the hourglass, the eternal flight of time. Earlier I said that we were proud that time passed so fast and that we were catching up with the fast-spinning world. Here we go back to slow time, hourglass time, which puts us into a meditative state about speed, space, city, and our own heartbeats. But there is more to it. Let us go back once again to alchemical thinking.

FIGURE 33. Laura Vinci, *Hourglass*

Sand is the childhood of cement. Mixing sand, water, and cement powder yields the plastic substance with which we create to our own image our buildings, like God creating man out of clay. Cement is therefore the modern equivalent of biblical clay, the *prima materia*. With that substance we ended up creating monstrosities. In this art piece we are thrown back to the beginning, because if cement were put into the blender—to stay with kitchen symbolism—the end result would be sand again. We have to acknowledge that this is what the alchemical imagining of the city is saying: "Change your attitude and go back to the beginning. Turn cement back into sand again. There you have a second chance to build something reasonable. Do not forget to put in a little mercury this time. Do not forget to let air circulate through the mixture. Try again." This is what the unconscious, through alchemy, is saying.

For us therapists there is an interesting analogy to be made here. Dora Kalff, in her talks with Jung, developed a technique of healing called sandplay therapy, in which the patients use sand as the support for miniatures that give shape to inner, sometimes unconscious, figures.[4] In that kind of therapy, working with sand would give patients a second chance to structure a more genuine personality. The sand in a decayed mill could then be used to shape a new urban environment, taking into account all that we have learned in the last one hundred years of psychotherapy.

Next we entered an empty room, from whose derelict windows we could see, on one side, the industrial sector, and from the other, the intricate cobweb of downtown skyscrapers. The artist, Eliane Prolik (*Bread Dough*), randomly laid out electrical cables on the floor, with several lit lightbulbs. Then she arranged around the empty space some iron four-legged structures, upon which were flattened, thin pewter sheets. They looked like beds. And upon these pewter beds she deposited bread dough. The dough was left there, and soon it began to ferment. The smell was typical, and that was the image: bread dough upon hard metal beds. Artist as midwife: what creative symbolic idea and image have been born?

What is the unconscious attempting to say here? Bread is the primal food. Bread is a religious symbol. It is made out of wheat. We are in a decadent wheat mill. . . . Here we have bread dough, but we have no oven. So this bread cannot be baked. It cannot become food for the soul. I think the unconscious is saying, "You foolish people, you forget that you have to feed your soul with true bread and not with consumerism, illusions, and fast food but with essential food for body and soul."

For that we need an oven. The oven too belongs in alchemy. Inside it, controlled fire works transmutations, and in due time the bread will be ready to be eaten. Baking bread is a transformative process. We cannot eat it raw. Raw bread is a nonsense.

But that is not all. Depending on how you look at this scene, there appears the Freudian couch. If we go into that apparition, it would mean that unbaked bread dough has to go to the analyst to find out what is happening. So this is actually a beautiful image of cultural therapy. Perhaps Hayao Kawai would have liked this, because he believed that therapy should make people identify with a stone and forget about their ego.[5] What we have here is not personal therapy at all but city therapy. It so happens that the part of the city that is going to therapy is bread dough, which then would talk to somebody and report what it has been dreaming of lately, what its wishes and complaints are, and what it thinks is wrong with it. Why does it not succeed in transforming and becoming a good, normal loaf of bread? This bread therapy, I am convinced, would be more fruitful for the city than a plebiscite.

We now proceed to a room in which there is an artificial creek whirling around a gravel pathway (see figure 34). Gravel is a machine-processed building element and when mixed with cement helps it to be still harder. This is the only work in which there is a human figure. The artist had a black man, a model, pose nude for him. He then took pictures of this nude black man and had the care to place a whole series of portraits exactly in the same spot where the pictures were taken. That is all. Viewers followed the gravel pathway and saw different poses. If they were affected by it, they might then ask if there were such a man in alchemy.

Yes, he was called the Ethiopian.[6] Alchemy in Europe was a white pursuit, but it was born in Egypt. People there had dark skin. As has happened to African culture, many of its best creations went to white hands. Time passes, the origins are forgotten, and they no longer get the credit. In European alchemy, the Ethiopian, the black man, meant the shadow, the radical other, the unknown other man who dwells in ourselves. I am a white man; my other is a black man inside me. If we have racial prejudice it is because we have an equivalent inner racial prejudice against an unknown part of ourselves, usually represented

FIGURE 34. Willi Biondoni, *Photos of a Black Man*

by a black or an Indian. The alchemists said that we have to talk to the Ethiopian and come to terms with him. He is nude. He is not hiding himself. He has no persona to distance him. He is there ready for us. Go to him. Listen to him. Start a relationship with him. This room is therefore an initiation chamber, such as those in Pompeii, those villas with allusive frescoes painted on their walls. This is a contemporary initiation room, in which city dwellers have to meet the other, the deep other in themselves.

We moved on in the exhibit to a Helio Melo's *Shoe Shop*. The art consisted of a collection of single shoes, not the pair, hanging on the wall. A few were scattered randomly on the floor. Different kinds of shoes were chosen, and there we could start our flow of associations. Many of us would think of a shoe shop or a shoe repair shop. I remember when I was a boy that if there were a hole in my shoe's sole, I would go to the shoe repair shop on the corner and have it repaired. There were always a few that the owners forgot to claim. That was a tradition. After a month the owner would lose the property of his unclaimed shoe. What has this prosaic detail have to do with alchemy? Here we have dirty tennis shoes, old high-heel shoes, executive shoes, sandals, baby shoes. The first alchemical metaphor here is one-sidedness. We cannot have just one foot or one shoe. We need two. Otherwise we will become one-sided and consider reality only from one side. We must work on this dangerous collective attitude by searching for the missing shoe. The shoe shop scene also brings to mind car accidents, when a single shoe is lost in the middle of the highway.

Thinking of the grave problems created by one-sidedness, we can go back to our previous discussion of the interplay between the masculine and the feminine principles. I have discussed the psychological and historical distortions caused by the monopoly of an unbridled phallic principle. An equivalent disaster would occur if the feminine principle ran unchecked in a similar way. One principle controls and balances the other—that is the old wisdom. So, I would say, the feminine principle should bridle the masculine and vice versa. They should not run wild, nor should one dominate or overrun the other. What would a city ruled by an unrestrained feminine principle be like? It would be absolutely chaotic too. Such cities do not exist now, if they ever did, because we are historically patriarchal, but it would be just the opposite. Something would be missing, perhaps Logos as we know it, goal-oriented projects, or something of the sort. We are always in the middle of the crash between two opposites, although we know more about the masculine principle than about the feminine, because this one has been repressed for so long. Actually, I do not really know what an unbridled feminine principle is all about. I can imagine it, but I have never seen it. Some people talk about the matriarchy, and we sort of see it in the movies. But I do contend that, in this moment of time, we need more of the feminine. We have had enough of the masculine principle. It is exhausted. We need balance.

The unpaired dirty shoe also alludes to a dreadful image we all have kept somewhere in a corner of our memories—those piles of shoes taken away from the Jews at the ghetto before they were driven away to the concentration camps. Death is present in this scene. Some dimension of death is instilled in a community when there is no longer faith and hope. The kind of disease that affects our cities burdens the soul with the sadness of death.

São Paulo is full of idiotic stimulation. Images appear randomly and badly disturb the landscape. There is an overdose of blown-up printed scenes involving toothpaste, cell phones, cars, bras, computers, smiling women, couples playing with dogs, margarine, credit cards. All over. We are bombarded with advertising billboards, chaotic images, and fast food—a stream of sheer stupidity filling our visual field from all angles. Our eyesight can never rest, nor can it be inspired, amused, or instructed. Perhaps there could be symbols or poetry instead. In one work, the artist zoomed in on cheap dishes of food and hung those pictures as critical images (Rocheli Costa, *Photos of Food Dishes*). This is the kind of food that millions of people eat every day. An unheard, unconscious voice in the city seems to be asking, "Is this all we live for?" We spend our lives traveling three or four hours back and forth from home to work in a jammed bus, doing undignified work, being ill-treated by our bosses, getting poor checks at the end of the month, enduring all the curses of the city to have that dish of food as a reward? Is this all that there is to life? Nothing beyond mere survival?

FIGURE 35. Assemblance of debris by exhibit workers.

The Alchemy of Cement in a Modern City

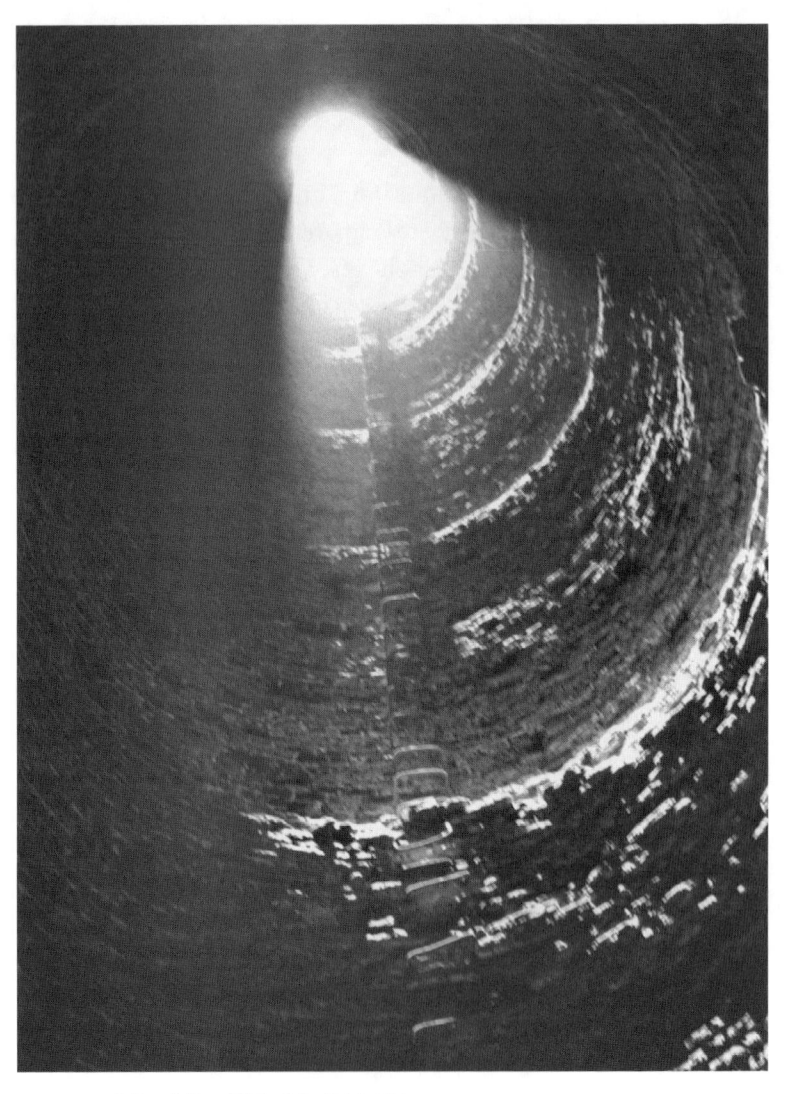

FIGURE 36. Jose Miguel Wisnick, *Brick Chimney*

Now we step outside (see figure 35). Workers, not artists, did this. They separated different kinds of debris—broken bricks, concrete fragments, roof tiles, dismantled wooden structures. Organization of chaos. One of the fundamental steps in alchemy before a new fusion takes place is *separatio*. We have to separate things inside ourselves. Some things are valuable and should be kept; some should be thrown away. Urban chaos reflects psychological chaos: one affects the other, but to grow out of it differentiation of what is what is needed. Alchemy is very paradoxical: sometimes mixing, sometimes separating. Sand would be cement going back to its origin. Here again we have a movement of going back to elementary building blocks. If an alchemical separation of the essences is achieved, then we can start to build again with psychologically recycled bricks, cement, gravel, stones, iron, water, and wood.

Going to see the last work, we walked on polluted soil covered with debris. The alchemists also called the *prima materia* the "bitter earth," a dead, acid soil from which something new might grow if the pain of transmutation is carried all the way through. Looking down, I noticed seedlings fighting their way upward to light and air. It was like an answer to all the uncomfortable questions raised by this strange art exhibit: life coming back to the surface again. And now, by Paulo Pasta, just a blue canvas on the back wall of another empty room, a window finally opened to the sky, to infinity, to spiritual transcendence. Instead of a cheap dish of food, it is blue as soul food.

To view the last work, visitors wore construction security helmets and entered a short tunnel leading inside a brick chimney (see figure 36). In the beginning of the industrial era, these chimneys were symbols of modernity. The only interference by the artist was to arrange wooden benches. This time, we could sit, relax, and look up to the sky through a round opening. And now comes the best part, the sound of flutes filling the whole space. At that point, one could feel something like this: "I am sitting inside a chimney out of which, in the past, the smoke of capitalism was released to dissolve in the air. But now, instead of a cloud of smoke, a cloud of music will spread over the city as a compassionate cloud of our love for it." Smog, at last, gave way to music.

ARTE/CIDADE (1997) was organized by Nelson Brissac Peixoto. Not all of the works in the exhibit have been commented on in this chapter.

CHAPTER 5

Bringing Soul Back to Education

DREAMS IN THE CLASSROOM

I have invited you to come along with me to look at newspapers with a different glance, to go back to the sixteenth century and re-imagine history, to walk on the streets of a megalopolis looking at suffering trees, and to visit an art exhibit in a derelict building with alchemy on our minds. Now we will go back to the earliest classroom in our educational system (to preschool and kindergarten), contact again that experience, and prepare ourselves to understand what can happen if education opens the door to the unconscious.

The idea of this chapter is that something can be done to bring soul back to education. This assumes that education has become soulless. However debatable this argument may be, it seems to me that education has no soul when it fails to arouse in children a love for knowledge or to encourage them to develop their creative potential. Children go to school because they have to, but it seems that passion is not in the classroom, not even in recreation. Teachers have become mother surrogates, sometimes negative mother figures who believe that they have a monopoly on knowledge, children being ignorant.

Some teachers seem to ignore that the best way to teach is to learn together. There is not enough room for imagination and creativity in a kind of education whose goal is to build fit citizens for the technological era.

In the second chapter I spoke briefly about Latin American history. Children are required to learn that subject in such an external and passive way that they do not get involved. There is no empathy and no fantasy. Their teachers would never say, "Now close your eyes, relax, and imagine you are an Indian having fun on the beach when all of a sudden you see this big brown vessel approaching. You have never in your life seen such a thing, and it carries strange-looking men with hair on their chins and shining adornments. Tell me now what you feel. What is going to happen? What the Indian and the explorers think, you and them, etc." This would be teaching history through imagination and not passive memorization. Children could be stimulated to bring forth their intuition, their capacity to see ahead and envision things that are not yet perceptible or conceived. Children are masters of imagination, but our school system combats precisely that on the wrong assumption that to educate a child is to remove him or her from the world of imagination and intuition and instead build and reinforce a rational ego. The technological myth is that only a clearcut, standard ego is able to absorb and organize knowledge, but that view is sterile.

We have to look carefully at this rational standpoint, which represents a power dispute between two perspectives: one maintains that only conscious ego rationality creates an efficient culture, and the other values the unconscious, creativity, and the spiritual Self, criticizing the identification between culture and technological progress. The first is a view that believes it is a theory; the second is a direct expression of the psyche in its multiplicity of functions. The theory of modern education has aligned itself with the first and has not yet been able to recognize how much a fiction it is. As now a growing awareness of the shortcomings of modern society points to education's one-sidedness, long-forgotten subjectivity is now fighting for its return. The ego-Self connection needs not to be ignored at school in order to promote human development.

Can we not conceive of a kind of education in which a child grows and maintains side by side: Self and ego, imagination and the sense of reality, reason and poetry, straight lines and curved lines, information and formation, thinking rationally and thinking intuitively? This question has led me to consider that education has ignored the findings of psychology, especially depth psychology, as if they were two rival siblings, which in fact they are, competing for space and time. Because education is older, it might be saying, "I am not interested in your findings. You have not convinced me with your insistence that there is an unconscious part of the psyche that has to be taken into account. I leave that for you, because you are the only one who believes in it." For the last one hundred years depth psychology has tried to understand this relationship between ego and Self, what belongs to each, the dialectic between these two poles, how one feeds or obstructs the other, the values and perspectives associated with each one. Depth psychology has acquired some knowledge about the function of symptoms, about the workings of the mind, about the mythological and religious layers of the psyche, about the connections between inner and outer worlds, psyche and soma, soul and ideas, about the language and importance of dreams and fantasies. Something definitive has been observed and gathered in the course of the last hundred years at least. Yet, probably due to a stern competition, for the most part education has turned its back on the strongest statements that the psychology of the unconscious has tried to make.

As a counter-reaction, psychologists became quite inflated, developed an irritating jargon that is always indicative of intellectual insecurity, and claimed that they knew more, more profoundly, and better. The other group replied, "I will simply ignore you." The overall result of this splitting of approaches is that the word *unconscious* is absent in the whole work of Piaget, and the *Encyclopedia of Psychoanalysis* assembled by Laplanche and Pontalis omits an entry for *intelligence*. How can intelligence and the unconscious be kept in separate boxes? We know that intelligence springs from an archetypal, unconscious matrix that prepares the mind to function in a certain way, because it certainly can function in other ways, different from what we call "normal." It has been demonstrated that an unconscious thinking process has

PLATE 1

PLATE 2

PLATE 3

PLATE 4

PLATE 5

PLATE 6

PLATE 7

PLATE 8

PLATE 9

PLATE 10

PLATE 11

PLATE 12

PLATE 13

PLATE 14

PLATE 15

PLATE 16

helped physicists and mathematicians, not to speak of poets and artists, to break through the prevailing paradigm of scientific knowledge and make important discoveries.[1] Quantum physics has definitively established that there is no absolutely objective knowledge. The act of observing an external object is filtered by a subjective screen and at the same time interferes with the very condition of the object. There is always an unknown factor collaborating with our conscious efforts to obtain knowledge or to create images that give substance to our culture. We have come to accept the difficult fact that the unconscious has an intelligence of its own. It has its own purposes and goals, and the best thing we can do is to create a bridge between the two realms, putting an end to an ignorant arrogance that insists on recognizing the reality of just one side. If the school tries to keep these two rivers apart and succeeds, children are taught to become split people, because it was ignored that at the root of true knowledge there must be an unconscious predisposition to learn. The archetype, or unconscious pre-existing matrix, that sustains the whole edifice of education is denied as non-existent. Consequently, even the most efficient pedagogic technique will not be able to ignite the soul.

If I have a dream of, say, a tree, my unconscious is indicating that there is a readiness in me to accrue some knowledge, or experience, connected with trees. I am sensitized, or—to use a photographic metaphor—my personal film is ready to receive an impression, and it is up to me to facilitate that or not, to leave it to chance, or to go for it. The best educational program would be one that runs parallel to the changing unconscious constellations in the psyches of the students. Instead, we have standard and official programs that establish precisely, like a straight line, what a seven-year-old child has to learn during the year, regardless of unexpected openings to the absorption and development of other interests. The Tree of Knowledge is homogenized. It is turned into a cement tree; its branches can no longer follow the wind. Sometimes, at age seven, children are ready to learn some astronomy, but because they cannot yet write correct Portuguese, this handicap has to be worked out first. Astronomy must wait—probably until after the interest disappears, perhaps never to return. The branch that could not develop for lack of water will certainly not reappear later in life. Maybe these children had astronomy constellated in their unconscious and could have intuitively understood extremely complicated phenomena having to do with the space-time continuum. Why should these children be denied something for which their unconscious is indicating they are ready? It is because there is an insurmountable separation between education and the psychology of the unconscious; however, in the living person that separation still does not exist. As far as I know, it has never occurred to school principals that simple and inexpensive experiments in this area can be pursued by just listening to children's dreams.

In 1997 I started a project, "Dreams in the Classroom." I was invited by Eda Canepa and Jeannette DeVivo to lecture at a private school about the relationship between education and the unconscious. I mentioned how often Jung stated that dreams taught him things that he was not able to formulate. As an example, I told them about his famous dream in which he saw the several layers of a house, each historically older than the other, and how that image made him understand the structure of the psyche from a surface, individual dimension to a deep, unknown, collective layer that he then called collective unconscious. His *Memories, Dreams, Reflections* recounts dozens of dreams from which Jung learned, among other things, that he should research alchemy or differentiate the reality of the Self from ego consciousness—a dream in which he sees a Yogi in meditation.[2] As I followed this train of thought, an idea started to take shape, and then, out of the blue, I proposed that the school schedule a time for children ages three to six to tell their dreams in the classroom, once a week, in front of their teacher and classmates. Once this idea was formulated, the rest followed quite naturally.

The initial proposal stipulated that the teacher write each dream verbatim on a sheet of paper if the child were still unable to do it alone, and then the child would draw the dream on the other side. That was all. No teacher was obligated to do it unless she (all were females) felt personally motivated to do so, nor was she to follow any kind of manual as to how to proceed. I proposed that we do an experiment and therefore follow the rules of research methodology, namely, observation, annotation, repetition of the observation, re-formulation and correction of hypotheses, and gathering and classification of the empirical material. Only then could we start to theorize about what was happening. We have been doing that regularly since then, and now we have more than ten thousand dreams and drawings. I am deeply grateful to the fifty or so teachers who believed in this project and worked on it with great dedication, openness, and creativity.

Let me first tell you the kinds of questions that arose when I started working with the teachers. One of the first questions was, "But what do we do with the dreams?" I said, "You listen to them. You let each child speak, let the others listen, and then we will see what comes up." Then another said, "But, excuse me, I was not trained to be a psychotherapist." And I replied, "I am not saying that you have to act as a psychotherapist nor that you will have to acquire new technical knowledge. You have a potentiality for a new approach, of which you are not aware, and we will attempt to bring it forth. Dreams are not the property of psychology. We analysts do not have a monopoly over dreams. We are not the only experts. From time immemorial humanity dealt with dreams in a variety of different ways. Shamans always used dreams; prophets, spiritual guides, wise elders, poets, and artists knew what to do with dreams. Why not teachers? Anybody can use a dream for purposes other than treating a patient in therapy. Analyzing dreams in therapy is just one use that can be made, and, by the way, it turns out to be a very good one. We have tested it over the last one hundred years. It works most of the time. There are different schools that say dreams are this or that, that people should or should not interpret them, that there is a right interpretation and people should know it, while another school would disagree. Jungian psychoanalysts use dreams to treat people who are somehow out of balance; for us it is a useful working tool. However, that does not mean that someone else cannot use dreams for other purposes and develop other methods and other approaches." I sensed that the teachers could do it—and they did.

We have been carrying on this *experiment* for four years. Why do I emphasize the term experiment? First, because we do not have any prior theory; second, because we have no certainties; third, because we have to observe and evaluate results; fourth, we have to develop a know-how; and fifth, in experiments it is possible to go wrong—that is part of it. If we realize something is not well thought out we can think it over again. An experiment means an open work, no certainties but insights, and sound empirical observation following the rules of scientific methodology, but with intuition, too.

After we started, I was soon summoned to meet with the teachers because they were very anxious. They complained, "We think this is dangerous, because the dream images are so threatening, so weird. We fear that by doing this dream experiment we might touch some latent psychotic nucleus in the children, and this could make them crazy and do damage to them. We do not know how to deal with that. The parents will complain, and they can even sue us." I said, "I give you my word that listening to children's dreams can never be harmful to them. If a child has a psychotic nucleus, a dream report will not activate it, and it might even help the child by indicating that some care must be taken with that particular child. A dream might warn us that some disruption is about to happen. We can then direct that child to a therapist preventively, on the basis of the evidence provided in the dream. Also, a terrible dream or nightmare could indicate a problem that could then be dealt with by getting the child into mental health care." At that point, without any prior experience, they had to believe me or just forget the project. After four years that anxiety is gone, because not a single child in a group of four hundred became psychotic as a result of our experiment. No children got out of control, lost their (mental) footing, or mixed reality with fantasy. As predicted, a few children in need were referred for treatment on the basis of disturbing dreams.

We had started with a declared fear of dream images. I insisted, "You have been teaching children for more than twenty years. You are not familiar with their dream images, and the first time you see them you are afraid? Do you think it would be better not to know these images? Do you not listen to your son's and daughter's dreams? How can you educate children if you are afraid of their inner world? That is an incomplete education." After all, what were those frightening images? Sharks, dinosaurs, super-heroes, whales, witches, holes, bats, robbers, mother is dying, father disappears, brother is born as an animal, grandmother is no longer there to be seen, darkness, blood, knives, spiders. I told them, "Did you not know that children live in the mythological world? Children are living the hero archetype from ages three or four onward, and therefore they have to meet the dinosaur and fight with the big snake. There is more action in their dreams than in a Spielberg movie. This is why they enjoy these kinds of movies so much. They reflect their dreams, which are still even more creative. They watch movies to be assured that what they imagine exists out there and that they are not crazy. So let us go to their inner cinema and be their companion. We want to know the contents of their dreams. These children do not need to be treated; they just need to be heard."

The first noteworthy thing at the start of the experiment was that children were not afraid and immediately accepted what was being offered. Many introverted boys and girls, who were usually afraid to open their mouths and express themselves in the classroom, when asked to tell their dreams for the first time, became protagonists, the center of attention. They had been regarded by classmates as silly or dumb but all of a sudden had something quite interesting to say. This fact alone affected the group dynamics. Some children were leaders because they were strong or extroverted, but with this dream-telling experiment another side of their personalities came to the fore. Children began to know themselves and each other better and in different ways. Soon they invented a fantastic game. As they liked to play with each other's toys, they began playing with each other's dreams. One child would say to another, "Can I go into your dinosaur dream? I am in your dream with you, and I want to take part in it myself." They would invite each other to play in each other's dreams, as they did when they invited other children to their homes. Are not dreams homes too?

Another important thing was that the dreams had to be written. Those who were beginning to write felt a new motivation, because now they had the goal of writing their own dreams. Teachers noticed an improvement in writing skills, most likely because the children believed that it was their own text and not something taken from a book. These children took a test traditionally used in that school to measure readiness for learning and writing the alphabet, and for the first time there was an upgrade in the usual scores. Other children developed their capacity to draw. They were inhibited before and allegedly would not draw, but when asked to express inner images they would draw in a completely new way. The spontaneity of those drawings, as you will soon see, is amazing, and there is no interference whatsoever from the teachers.

Furthermore, the teachers believed that they were discovering their pupils. For example, they said: "Now I understand why Tom was restless all the time and why Jane was so gloomy. I understand why last week Johnny was behaving in a certain way and now he has changed, because it is all in his dreams." Sometimes a child goes to school, enters the daily ritual, and the teacher is completely ignorant of central psychological facts, like mom and dad went away to Europe for a month. Tina goes to school, sits lost in a world of potent fantasies that her parents will not return, and the teacher just says, "Pay attention!" How can Tina pay attention if last night in her dream she saw two balloons carrying her parents up and disappearing in the sky? How can Bob put aside the hard fact that his turtle died and that he is now wondering if it had a soul and that it might return as a fish. He is also thinking that he should have buried it or written its name on a stone. This is where Bob is, but the teacher is talking about grammar. Can she not for a little while also talk about life and death, rebirth, soul, and funeral rituals? If the teachers were connected to dream motifs and fantasies, they would have a new criterion to select topics for discussion. The teachers would then be addressing a vital concern in a specific child, and the whole classroom would benefit.

Teachers have to follow a course program, but there is some freedom left. This is what was used creatively in this experiment. The idea was to pick a subject that was recurring or prevalent at that time but that usually would not be considered appropriate. For instance, these topics emerged from the children's dreams: what does one feel or fantasize when mommy is pregnant, when parents get divorced, when grandma dies, when someone is angry with you. Another important topic for conversation was the school and the teacher's shadow. Both the dangerous side of the school and the nasty side of the teacher appear in the pupils' dreams. Schools do engage in long meetings to achieve self-evaluation, but if they really want to do it they might consider the way their shadow appears in those dreams. We will see some of them.

Now that we have thousands of dreams we must decide how to store them, and for that criteria are needed. Also, I believed that we needed to organize the material according to some prevalent topics. An unexpected reaction was that teachers became interested in noting their own dreams and in studying not dream interpretation but dream symbolism. They started with Gaston Bachelard and are now beginning to read some of Jung's seminars and the works of Joseph Campbell.[3] As a result of their involvement, they developed an approach of their own, organizing a file for each child, detecting recurrent patterns, looking at whole series of dreams and recognizing each child's style, and noticing, through dreams, that a certain child must have had some problem that week—so they asked and talked about it. Instead of using psychological concepts and jargon, they have been making comments like, "I think Ted is stuck, but he may overcome it now, because last week there was this image in his dream in which such and such happened." When doing that, teachers are not competing with the school psychologist, nor feeling insecure about a discipline they have not studied. On the contrary, they are speaking based on evidence with which they are in close contact. That is the source of their new knowledge. It is clear now: dreams can be used as a tool to improve the capacity to learn, both for children and their teachers. All learn together. The archetype is no longer split between all knowledge on one side and all ignorance on the other.

This experiment is being carried out in an upper-middle-class school, attended exclusively by privileged, white children. My hope is to take this project to public schools and do exactly the same thing. All the teachers I have been talking about, who can do their work under good conditions, have agreed to pass on the know-how we have developed to teachers in the public system. If and when that happens, it will be possible to compare dreams of children in different social classes. Do children living in ghettoes or slums have the same or different dream motifs? Nobody, to my knowledge, has researched this. I know for sure that dream structures will be the same, but I predict that motifs will change. Because there are so many variables involved, researchers could examine psychological, sociological, or anthropological issues using that material. Perhaps we could start projects in other countries and do national comparisons. I believe that this would be a sound way to use Jungian psychology to bring soul back to education.

Now let us listen to the children's dreams and look at their drawings. In the beginning I saw no order in this material, but gradually different categories came to the surface by themselves. We will go into each one of them. I remind you that this classification is a first attempt; new headings can and will be adopted. Also, the same dream might belong to more than one category.

Family and Home

A three-year-old boy's philosophical dream opens our series: "The one in green is my dog, and the other is my mother. I am a baby in her belly. She was sunbathing and having a glass of fruit juice. I dreamt I was inside my mother's belly when I was a baby" (see color plate 1). He drew himself in the womb in black, and in green his mother holding a big glass with two ice cubes. The smiling sun occupies the center of the sheet. This boy is beginning to think about origins, and he already knows that he has been inside his mother's belly. It cannot be affirmed that he also knows how he got in there, or how he came out. Here we have a good example of a sound process of becoming conscious through efficient thinking (the smiling sun), the early search for an answer to the mystery of life. If not interfered with, this is a natural process for children and corresponds to an organization of logical thinking from its unconscious matrix in fantasy. The dream, therefore, helps the boy to build his own knowledge. The important point, in this case, is the possibility of presenting the question in front of the teacher and classmates, bringing up this topic for legitimate discussion in the classroom.

A four-year-old girl dreamt that she was a red flower. Her father was a sunflower, and her mother, a daisy. They were in the same garden but her parents' stems had been cut. We could ask what is happening with the parents or follow another track and realize that in this drawing full of vitality this girl is giving expression to an important psychological fact: her unconscious has decreased her parents' importance and increased her own, reinforcing her growing process and her ego without the interference of too-strong parental figures. Here we can see how a dream like this supports the ego, contrary to the old belief that through education ego and imagination should be kept apart.

I compared two dreams by the same three-year-old girl. This caption accompanied one of the drawings: "It was raining; the water washed away all the little plants in my home and then they faded." Lower, six months later: "I was taking a walk with my mother and then a monster appeared in the middle of the way." Rain, for this girl, appears not in its creative aspect to promote growth, but to destroy what has been achieved. The appearance of the monster, in this context, is very disquieting. The teacher does not have to be a therapist to use these two dreams as an indication that this girl must be undergoing some emotional difficulty at home. Perhaps her mother is pouring a rain of hard criticism over her feelings. Once they were encouraged to do so, teachers quite naturally began to pay closer attention to children having this kind of dream. They gradually became familiar with difficult situations of young children. This new access to their pupils' subjectivity made them feel that they were now looking at them from a different angle. This girl cannot be properly evaluated in her school performance leaving her two dreams out of the picture.

These are two dreams by a four-year-old girl. The lower drawing illustrates this scene: "I was in the sea and there was a whale who became my friend. I was with my father and his girlfriend" (see color plate 2). The parents are going through a separation, and the father already has a new companion. We can see the whale in the center, and in the sky what seems to be her apartment building, with herself, perhaps, in the window. We could say that she is standing at left, followed by her father, wearing a hat, and another woman. At right, a man, also wearing a hat, shoots at the whale. Note that this dramatic episode is in the drawing, but not in the dream text. Is father hurting the mother image for this girl? Is the upper part of the drawing, with a heart, a comet, and a dark spot opposite the sun, trying to compensate for the pain portrayed below? The dream above reads: "There was a hen and she was laying eggs. I was swimming in a swimming pool." She has not drawn the hen but three women, one very small, and several eggs, three being red and the rest black. Hen and whale can be seen as mother figures. If the first is friendly but hurt, the second is mothering and might procreate. Dark clouds hover over her name in the sky. We do not know if anybody is trying to help this girl who has to go to school carrying this drama inside her, but it is clear that the unconscious is doing its work, giving her images through which she can contact her deep feelings. In the future, because all these drawings are copied and the originals returned to the children at the end of the year, this girl will be able to look again at these images and perhaps understand what she was going through when she was four.

Now we have a dream—a drawing and text written by the boy himself—that serves as important evidence of the connection between writing and self-expression (see color plate 3). Writing here takes on the same quality as drawing, and this fact had never been observed before in the school. The practice of narrating dreams therefore stimulates both drawing and writing. In the lower part, four ducks are floating on the sea, and the text reads: "I dreamt that I was aboard, the ship turned over and I fell into the sea with my family." In the drawn image there is no ship and no shipwrecks. Turned into a family of ducks, all are afloat. If this dream is indicating the presence of some turmoil inside the family (the ship capsized), we can see in it, at the same time, how in his psyche this boy finds reassurance.

Let us consider a last dream in this "Family and Home" series, told and drawn by a five-year-old boy: "I dreamed that my mother was home and she threw a spider out of my window" (see color plate 4). The apartment building, its floors and windows, plus the spider, are all represented in the drawing. In my view, this suggests the hypothesis—if I take the spider as a symbol of autonomous negative fantasies that cause fear or night terrors—that this boy's mother, or his inner mother as we therapists would say, appears in her constructive dimension and actually helps him to get rid of some of his fears. If this is so, the dream would be indicating an unconscious process whereby impediments to growth are being resolved. If fear appears in the classroom, and the teacher related it to this dream, she might encourage the boy to dare more and overcome it, trusting that he is ready for it.

School

The first dream is told by a child who just turned three: "I dreamt that I was in school and on the teacher's bookshelf there was a real baby.

Then my friend Louise screamed at me, saying that I couldn't take the baby with me because it was hers. Then I left the baby on the bookshelf and didn't take it home with me. Then I woke up" (see color plate 5). This dream allows us to believe that the experiences this girl is having at school have facilitated her development, because she is already able to leave behind the baby that she has been. A dream such as this should be taken as a parameter for this girl's evaluation, together with other kinds of traditional indicators. If teachers understand this language of dreams, they will perceive the opposite situation, when a child finds emotional difficulties in growing. They could then search for the negative impact that the school milieu is—or they are—having on that child.

Another one, by a six-year-old boy: "I dreamt with an alien. I was in school, a flying saucer appeared and then I had a fight with them. I was the only one clever enough to do it. Then I woke up" (see color plate 6). This boy sees himself as a hero in school, courageous enough to combat unknown enemies because he is in possession of his cleverness, and he has the chance to use the word "alien," which is not common parlance. He does not identify the separate characters in his drawing. In other words, maybe some children do feel that they are aliens until they reach a definite self-image. As a hero, this boy is perhaps affirming his ego identity against fantasies of inadequacy. If this assumption is true, his dream is a clue both to the teacher as how to deal with him, and to himself, as a boy growing strong.

A five-year-old girl had a dream that referred to a hidden problem in the school: "I dreamt that I cut my finger here in the school with a blade. I like the dreams I have, but not this one. They changed the sand pool, instead of a rectangle, it was oval. We didn't know there were little holes in the sand. Vivian and Julie cut their fingers in the little hole, but I didn't see the blood" (see color plate 7). If the school principals want to work on the school's shadow, they should study this dream. In her dream, the girl realizes that something hidden on the playground causes harm to her and her classmates. One of the girls in the drawing has no arms, at left we see razor blades, and at right, amputated hands stuck in the ground. Cutting one's finger or having to show fingers to the witch is a classical image in fairy tales. Criticism sometimes cuts as a blade, castrating spontaneity, or the will to act. Fingers are essential for writing, drawing, and other manual works. In this case, it is up to the school to reveal where the witch is hiding. The girl cannot do that alone.

Growth

This topic appears in simple dream reports such as, "The other day I went alone to the playground in my building, called my friend, and in the end I swam alone because he didn't follow me." One part of him is afraid to go out unaccompanied and plunge into his new experiences, but he identifies with the resolute part that has courage and initiative. It is probable that when this dream was shared the boy felt proud of himself. Growth is constellated in the unconscious, so the pupil might respond positively to stimuli involving new habits and leaving behind infantile fixations.

A certain teacher noted that during a math class a shy six-year-old girl, who up until then had not shared any dream, came to her and said that she wanted to tell a dream right then. The teacher called the attention of the class, the ongoing activity was interrupted, and the girl related the following story: "I dreamt that I was inside a back-sack, then I stuck my head out, cried for help, but to no avail because my mother was sleeping" (see color plate 8). Then she proceeded to draw the scene: she is closed inside the sack and her head is not out. Her mother is asleep in a square and is caught by four crossed lines, a double "no." The teacher is not her therapist, so she is not asked to interpret anything, but the scene itself, besides the way in which the dream was told, is a cry for help. I have asked the teachers to pay special attention to dreams in which there is an indifferent, careless, or right away non-caring mother figure. Because they naturally carry a mother projection and are to a certain degree mother substitutes—although they are not trained to understand thoroughly the nature of this role—teachers tend to think that maybe they should provide to such children something they are not getting from their own mothers. To be kept inside a backpack, generally used to carry books, suggests oppression, loss of freedom, perhaps a difficulty to do homework. Maybe the girl is afraid of the world and wants to hide in some safe, womb-like place, and her dream says, "No mother's help. Either you stay in the backpack, or you come out by yourself." The fact is that both the dream and the drawing are expressing something that this girl would be unable to verbalize.

A four-year-old boy had two separate dreams in which the question of courage toward reality and fantasy was distinctly formulated. The first dream: "I dreamt that there was a monster in the terrace, but he was wearing a costume. He was not a real ghost, but a person wearing a mask." This is another aspect of the question of growing, namely, the distinction between real and imaginary fears. This image contains the whole dynamics of fear: is it a mask or a monster? The second dream: "I dreamt that there was a monster on my terrace, and he was not disguised, it was a real monster. It was dark, I was not dreaming and went to my mother's bedroom." The drawing is very revealing (see color plate 9). The false monster is represented by the labyrinth of imagination, a pure fiction made of a thread of thoughts, and the real one, by a concrete weird head, that is, a truly felt fear. Discriminating what is and what is not, in other words, growing psychologically, is not an easy task. Here we see that it is the dream, not the school, that is teaching this boy this complex lesson.

Another interesting situation is presented by a dream in which a five-year-old boy discriminates between freedom from parental authority and limits imposed from within his own psyche. In his dream, he argues with the whole family and decides to sleep alone outside, inside a tent in the building's entrance lobby. It does not work out, because he hurts his head on the hard floor. His grandfather then appears and tells him that he should not do that. The dream puts him in a situation of self-examination, and for him that is where growth is, not in premature independence.

We could postulate the hypothesis that each step in the process of growing is worked, commented, or stressed by the unconscious, and this experiment gives us a wealth of material to check it. Take for instance the difficult moment of leaving behind the habit of sucking a pacifier. A four-year-old girl reported the following in her class: "I dreamt that I was sucking my pacifier, and then I told this to my cousin Peter, who also does it. He then said that dreams are true." We think it is a behavioral training on the part of parents or teachers to change that habit, but for the child it is a *deep* problem that has to be worked inside.

A five-year-old girl portrayed herself with an open smile, in complete happiness, her hands and feet looking like flowers (see color plate 10). And that was because in her dream she was going to the toy store all by herself. All the shelves at left are filled with red toys, which she can grab with her flower hands. Here we have an indication that the road ahead is open for this girl; she has pleasure in what she does and is proud of her courage to go after her objects of desire. She does not need mom as an intermediary to reach what makes her happy. Parents and teachers should become familiar with dreams that depict a state of well-being in children to have a pattern of comparison when something is going wrong.

Just one more example of a self-regulatory activity of a child's psyche. The drawing is the dream text, in Portuguese, which I translate: "I was driving and then I did not know how to brake and then I hit the car and I died" (see color plate 11). The pedals can be seen at left. So what is the problem with this three-year-old boy? He goes on and on and on, following his impulse, until he crashes with some obstacle. The part of him that does this has to die; he has to learn how to gain control over himself. But this is not behaviorism, it is the voice of a dream informing us that a mechanism of self-restraint is at work.

The Witch

We will now look at three dreams, all reported by girls. The first, by a six-year-old: "One night I went to sleep and then a witch appeared and cut my hand off." The accompanying drawing (see color plate 12)—we have already noted how often the drawings complement the dream text—emphasizes not the amputated hand, which in fact does not appear, but instead the witch's tool, a cutting device, represented three times. In the place of the hand are organized blood stains. This girl, through her dream eye, is attempting to understand the negative mother's power to curtail her actions. She is collecting evidence of how many times she is affected. We could presume that, because she is studying and amplifying the weapon used against her, she is trying to find out how to disarm her opponent. The teacher was warned, to her great surprise, that she herself might be playing the witch role—her professional shadow—and so the matter should be carefully studied.

Parallel to the report mentioned above, in which the boy tried to distinguish between a false and a true monster, a girl turning six goes through the same experience: "I dreamt that I was watching TV and there was this witch movie and a guy with a bent head. Then both came out of the screen and I was frightened." She drew the television screen with a face, the two characters within a larger frame and then herself, armless, smashed against a chair (see color plate 13). The terrible figures are entering her three-dimensional world. She cannot avoid confronting them, but her fear makes her powerless. This girl's situation differs greatly from the one who examines the witch's cutting device. She is not yet ready to deal with a negative emotional scene in which she feels powerless.

Another girl, age five and a half, recounts: "I was dreaming in my bed and then this witch came; she tied me to a chair and was going to cook me in her pot, but then my father stepped in; he rescued me and took me home." She drew the scene in the moment before her father's arrival, when she was alone in the house with the witch (see color plate 14). It might be argued theoretically that the father can play a decisive role in this witch-girl relationship, if the girl does not possess her own resources. Being tied to a chair suggests immobilization, and quite often the mother's animus does that if a child does not eat or do homework properly. Working with adults, we have learned the kinds of marks those early punishments sometimes leave. It might also indicate excessive containment, inhibition, or prohibition of action, expansion, or spontaneity.

Animals

A three-year-old boy's dream was collected in the first week of the experiment. The teacher wrote the text in the drawing: "I was trying to run away, and then he bit me and then I kicked him." He who? "A shark." And as a parallel, a boy the same age related: "In my dream an enormous earthworm coiled around me and caught me." He shows us how completely he was immobilized—only his head was out (see color plate 15). As we have seen different reactions by three girls to a witch, here one boy first tries to run away but then confronts the dangerous shark, whereas the other cannot prevent the big worm from paralyzing him. Although the boys are the same age, they have different ego configurations. When I came into contact with these dreams, it occurred to me that a bridge could be built between this dream experiment and experience art therapy. If these two boys, or the girls who were in different ways trying to confront their fear of the witch, could represent the shark and the big earthworm in clay or, even better, if they could interact dramatically with those creatures in a dance workshop, undoubtedly genuine emotions would manifest because of the link with unconscious material.

A six-year-old girl dreamt that her mother was pregnant, "but the baby was a hippopotamus. Then I was putting on a skirt, but inside it was full of ants. I was wondering if I should have my hair cut or not." In her drawing, the mother does not appear, only herself and her symbolic skirt. The girl drew the baby proportionately very small, because she views it as a strange hippo, that is, not her kind. Hardly would a child expecting a sibling be able to express with words all the subtleties of this typical situation, generally overlooked in school. It itches and irritates. The rival-to-be must not be human! Dreams here are more articulate than an educated ego, and that is exactly the reason why they should be heard.

The same problem appeared in another girl's dream. She was three and a half. First she saw two monkeys, then she went under the bed and heard a baby monkey crying. The threatening other, the future brother or sister, at this point is represented as an animal.

Heroes

It was found that a good number of boys, many more than girls, report dreams in which they play the part of heroes. That inner experience certainly corresponds to the gradual configuration of a sound, apt ego that will enable the child to cope with ever-changing circumstances in the environment. If dreams express that development, it makes no sense to defend a style of education that represses subjectivity and imagination and threatening dimensions for ego formation.

Here is a good example, by a five-year-old boy: "I was Superman and I attacked all the monsters. Ricky said I was a steel man." In his drawing, he knocked out the first monster of a row, but he still wrote the "R" of his name, Pedro, in reverse. A few weeks later, this same boy made another dream-drawing, but this time he wrote his "R" correctly, first smaller than the other letters, then big and clear. Overcoming this problem might in itself have been a heroic effort with success. The story is: "I became a basket-ball player and I called Spaceman and the Rabbit to play in my team. There were one hundred monsters. Rabbit hit the monster's head with the ball, made a score. The monsters died and we won." Fighting the monsters has rules, one can win the game, it is a matter of teamwork and cleverness. There are many dreams in this category, but because they mainly follow this structure, this example will suffice.

Death, Rebirth, Joy, and Transcendence

Children can have deep emotional experiences without even communicating to adults the extent of their feelings. A concise dream of a five-year-old girl expresses that in a most direct way: "I dreamt that my heart broke." Nobody needs to be trained to use that image as a clue to establish contact. A dream might refer to existential questions that would greatly surprise the assumptions commonly made by school professionals about what goes on in a child's mind. Take for instance the following, also by a girl, age six: "I dreamt that I was in the sea, then I got lost, sank, and died. Then I resurrected, and went on dying and resurrecting several times." It seems unbelievable that a small child is entertaining ancient ideas about life after death, rebirth, and reincarnation. These are all archetypal motives turned into dogmas by the great religions. People generally do not feel comfortable going into them as free-thinkers. In the following months, this girl reported an impressive series of highly symbolic dreams and drawings, later collected and exhibited on a large panel in her classroom.

Certain dreams refer to feelings and not so much to a dramatic plot or an image. For instance: "I dreamt that I was so happy," or "My dream is well kept, and it had three colors," or "I dreamt that I am a fairy." A three-year-old reported: "I dreamt that I was an angel in Heaven. Then I turned my head down and woke up." These dreams convince me of the empirical foundations of Jung's ideas concerning the archetypes in the collective unconscious. After some negative projections that keep us from recognizing the profound perceptions of children are withdrawn, we now have some impressive evidence of descriptions made by children about the origin and nature of the soul and its relation with God and the whole of Creation. In his dream, a three-year-old boy can live his angel dimension, but life on Earth calls him back down here.

I will close this chapter with the most unexpected of all dreams, told by a six-year-old boy: "I was alone in the desert, and I saw a light. I followed it. I came to a tent, which was lit from inside, and there I was to meet God. But can you imagine? He did not shake hands with me. So, in the end, I could not see his face. Maybe it was not God at all." The image he drew consisted of two hearts, half green and half blue, and an abstract form as a kind of hand (see color plate 16). This school provides no religious teaching of any kind, but this boy is dreaming the fundamental question of Western theology: Can man see God? In his unconscious dimension, the dreamer lived an uncommon experience being in a desert and following a light. However, this is a common experience of spiritual leaders. The doubt as to the reality of that experience is at the center of our culture and not at all his personal problem. How do we know if we have been in God's tent in the desert? Maybe it is an invention. Maybe it is true. How do we know? Must we believe in something we do not know? Or can we know? When the BBC reporter asked Jung, "Do you believe in God?" Jung answered, "Believe? I don't need to believe. I know." This boy is working on the same problem Jung worked all his life, and he drew man and God as two separate entities, or two colors in the same heart: blue referring to the spiritual or transcendent dimension and green to the concrete aspect of nature and man. This boy's drawing is saying that the heart is the place where these two dimensions meet. Only in the heart can they be felt and understood as being one.

When these children enter the first grade there is no longer a dream experiment to allow them to share their inner visions. The process is interrupted, because other school officials responsible for that section thought it might be harmful to an education that seeks to prepare young citizens to be successful in their future careers. Nevertheless, each child upon graduation from kindergarten takes home a folder with all the dreams told and drawn during the experiment. I believe this to be a priceless document of the soul that can only grow in significance as time goes by.

NOTES

Foreword

1. J. Sams and D. Carson, *Medicine Cards: The Discovery of Power Through the Ways of Animals* (Santa Fe: Bear & Company, 1988), pp. 76–79.
2. D. H. Rosen, *Transforming Depression: Healing the Soul Through Creativity* (York Beach, Maine: Nicolas-Hays, 2002).
3. Ibid.

Preface

1. This idea, first put forward in the psychological field by C. G. Jung, is brilliantly explained by Marie-Louise von Franz in chapter 9, "Reflexions," in *Projection and Re-collection in Jungian Psychology,* pp. 179–99. See also her chapter "Matter and Psyche from the Point of View of the Psychology of C. G. Jung" in *Psyche & Matter*.
2. See his chapter, "The Conjunction," in *Mysterium Coniunctionis,* especially paragraph 660: "While the concept of the *unus mundus* is a metaphysical speculation, the unconscious can be indirectly experienced via its manifestations. Though in itself an hypothesis, it has at least as great a probability as the hypothesis of the atom." In paragraph 663 we read: "*unus mundus,* the latent unity of the world."

Chapter 1

1. *Traité de l'homme*. Quoted by Alexander Roob in *Alchemy & Mysticism,* p. 572.
2. See C. G. Jung, *Psychology and Alchemy,* paragraph 356. *Lumen Naturae* means source of enlightenment.

3. See his "The Lambspring Figures" in *Jungian Psychiatry,* p. 290: "On the sea a complex (fish) with a dual aspect is constellated. It is the sort of psychic situation we find in people who are completely normal, kind, often cultivated, but unconscious of themselves. The complex has not yet revealed its true inner tension; the fish are identical."
4. See my *Indian Mirror,* p. 112, for the story of the German explorer Hans Staden, who in the end was not eaten by the Tupinambá Indians.
5. I have studied this very interesting phenomenon, but so far it has only been published in Portuguese. See my paper, "Os grandes temas arquetípicos na história da América Latina."
6. See her book, *The Cat—A Tale of Feminine Redemption,* p. 44: "this archetype is still on the rise, coming up over the horizon of the collective unconscious."
7. See *Aion,* paragraphs 147–49.

Chapter 2

1. See T. Todorov, *La Conquête de l'Amerique,* chapter three, p. 129.
2. See the front cover of this book.
3. See also my other papers on this subject in the bibliography.
4. See his *Transforming Depression,* chapter four, "Egocide and Transformation: a New Therapeutic Approach."

Chapter 3

1. See his essay, "The Philosophical Tree," paragraphs 304–482, in *Alchemical Studies.*
2. See his study on the tree, chapter ten in *L'Air et les Songes,* and on the root, chapter nine in *La Terre et les Reveries du Repos.*
3. *See his The Re-enchantment of Everyday Life,* chapter one, "Nature."
4. J. G. Neihardt, *Black Elk Speaks,* p. 230.
5. See Carlos Firkowski's paper, "Poluição Atmosférica e a Arborização Urbana," in *Anais do III Encontro Nacional sobre Arborização Urbana,* pp. 14–26.
6. Ibid.
7. See the paper by Rudi A. Seitz, "Considerações sobre a poda de árvores na arborização urbana," in *Anais do III Encontro Nacional sobre Arborização Urbana,* pp. 87–100.

Chapter 4

1. The Dallas Institute of Humanities and Culture was co-founded by James Hillman, Robert Sardello, and Gail Thomas in 1986.
2. "The Spirit Mercurius," *Alchemical Studies,* paragraphs 239–303.
3. I have used the Italian original version, *Crescita e Colpa.* See bibliography.
4. See her *Sandplay—A Psychotherapeutic Approach to the Psyche.*
5. See his *Buddhism and the Art of Psychotherapy.*
6. See Marie-Louise von Franz's lecture on the *Aurora Consurgens* in her *Alchemy: An Introduction to the Symbolism and the Psychology,* pp. 207–39. On page 210 it is said that "in alchemy the Ethiopian is often the symbol of the *nigredo* . . . negroes still turn up nowadays in the unconscious material of white people, namely the primitive, natural man in his ambiguous wholeness. The natural man in us is the genuine man, but also the man who does not fit into conventional patterns, and who in part is very much driven by his instincts." See also her commentary on the alchemical treatise *Aurora Consurgens,* p. 300 ff.

Chapter 5

1. See Marie-Louise von Franz, *Reflections and Re-Collections in Jungians Psychology,* chapter 3, "Projection and Scientific Hypotheses."
2. *Memories, Dreams, Reflections,* p. 323.
3. Bachelard's and Campbell's books—plus one by Fraser Boa—are mentioned in the bibliography. C. G. Jung, *Dream Analysis. Notes of the Seminar given in 1928–1930.*

BIBLIOGRAPHY

Anais do III Encontro Nacional sobre Arborização Urbana. Curitiba: FUPEF—UFPR, 1990.

Bachelard, Gaston. *La Terre et les Reveries du Repos.* Paris: Librairie José Corti, 1948.

———. *L'Air et les Songes.* Paris: Librairie José Corti, 1943.

———. *La Poétique de L'Espace.* Paris: Presses Universitaires de France, 1957.

Boa, Fraser. *The Way of Myth. Talking with Joseph Campbell.* Boston & London: Shambhala, 1994.

Campbell, Joseph. *The Power of Myth.* New York: Doubleday, 1988.

———. *The Mythic Image.* Princeton: Princeton University Press, 1974.

Fierz, H. K. "Diagnosis of the Individuation Process in Analysis: The Lambspring Figures," in *Jungian Psychiatry,* pp. 279–304. Einsiedeln: Daimon Verlag, 1991.

Gambini, Roberto. *Indian Mirror: The Making of the Brazilian Soul.* São Paulo: Axis Mundi/Terceiro Nome, 2000.

———. "A Formação da Alma Brasileira." *Anais do V Congresso Brasileiro de Psicopedagogia,* pp. 7–15. São Paulo: Vetor Editora, 2000.

———. "The Soul of Underdevelopment: The Case of Brazil." *Open Questions in Analytical Psychology. Proceedings of the Thirteenth International Congress For Analytical Psychology, Zurich, 1995,* pp. 139–48. Einsiedeln, Daimon Verlag, 1997

———. "O nascedouro da alma brasileira." *A Identidade Latino-Americana. Anais do II Congresso Latino-Americano de Psicologia Junguiana,* pp. 55–62. Rio de Janeiro, 2001.

———. "Sonhos na escola." *(Por) Uma Educação com Alma.* Ed. B. Scoz. Petrópolis: Editora Vozes, 2000.

———. "Os grandes temas arquetípicos na história da América Latina." *Anais do I Congresso Latino-Americano de Psicologia Junguiana,* pp. 45–65. Montevideo: Grafik-a, 2000.

———. "The Challenge of Backwardness," in *Post Jungians Today: Key Papers in Contemporary Analytical Psychology.* Ed. Ann Casement, pp. 149–62. London: Routledge, 1998.

———. "Portraits of Suffering Trees: Destruction of Nature and Transformation of Consciousness," in *Proceedings of the Fourteenth International Congress for Analytical Psychology—Florence '98.* Ed. M. A. Mattoon, pp. 199–207. Einsiedeln: Daimon Verlag, 1999.

Jung, C. G. *The Collected Works.* Princeton: Princeton University Press, 1969–70.
  Collected Works 9i, *The Archetypes and the Collective Unconscious,* "Archetypes of the Collective Unconscious."
  Collected Works 9ii, *Aion—Researches into the Phenomenology of the Self.*
  Collected Works 11, *Psychology and Religion: West and East.*
  Collected Works 12, *Psychology and Alchemy.*
  Collected Works 13, *Alchemical Studies.*
  Collected Works 14, *Mysterium Coniunctionis.*

———. *The Exercitia Spiritualia of St. Ignatius Loyola. Notes on the Lectures given at the E.T.H., Zurich, 1939–1940.* Mimeographed edition, with restricted circulation.

———. *Dream Analysis. Notes of the Seminar given in 1928–1930.* Ed. William McGuire. Princeton: Princeton University Press, 1984.

———. *Memories, Dreams, Reflections.* Recorded and edited by Aniela Jaffé. New York: Vintage Books, 1965.

Kalff, Dora M. *Sandplay: A Psychotherapeutic Approach to the Psyche.* Santa Monica: Sigo Press, 1980.

Kawai, Hayao. *Buddhism and the Art of Psychotherapy.* College Station: Texas A&M University Press, 1996.

Milano, Miguel, and Eduardo Dalcin. *Arborização de Vias Públicas.* Rio de Janeiro: Light, 2000.

Moore, Thomas. *The Re-enchantment of Everyday Life.* New York: HarperCollins, 1996.

Neihardt, J. G., ed. *Black Elk Speaks.* New York: Pocket Books, 1972.

Roob, Alexander. *The Hermetic Museum: Alchemy & Mysticism.* Köln: Taschen, 1997.

Rosen, David H. *Transforming Depression: Healing the Soul Through Creativity.* York Beach, Maine: Nicolas-Hays, 2002.

Ticuna Indians. *O Livro das Árvores.* Organized by J. G. Gruber. Benjamim

Constant: Organização Geral dos Professores Ticuna Bilíngües, 1997.

Todorov, Tzvetan. *La Conquête de l'Amérique: La Question de l'Autre.* Paris: Édition du Seuil, 1982.

von Franz, Marie-Louise. *Projection and Re-Collection in Jungian Psychology—Reflections of the Soul.* La Salle: Open Court, 1980.

———. *Alchemy: An Introduction to the Symbolism and the Psychology.* Toronto: Inner City Books, 1980.

———. *Psyche and Matter.* Boston & London: Shambhala, 1992.

———. *Aurora Consurgens. A Document Attributed to Thomas Aquinas on the Problem of Opposites in Alchemy.* London: Routledge & Kegan Paul, 1966.

———. *The Cat: A Tale of Feminine Redemption.* Toronto: Inner City Books, 1999.

Zoja, Luigi. *Crescita e colpa. Psicologia e limiti dello sviluppo.* Milano: Anabasi, 1993.

———. *Il gesto di Ettore. Preistoria, storia, attualità e scomparsa del padre.* Torino: Bollati Boringhieri, 2000.

INDEX

Color plates are indicated with pl., e.g. pl. 14.
Figures are indicated with *f*.

actress-mummy (newspaper images), 32
airplane dreams, 24
alchemy process: colors in, 89; elements of, 91–92, 103; green light, 20; principles of, 84; water, 89–90. *See also* art exhibit, symbols explored
Alexander VI (Pope), 42
"alien" dream (child's), 117, pl. 6
all-seeing eye archetype, 12
Amazon basin (newspaper image), 12
AmeriIndians. *See* Indians (American)
amputation dreams (children's), 117–18, 120–21, pl. 7, pl. 12
analyst's work. *See* depth psychology
ancestral father (European explorers), 48–52
ancestral mother (AmeriIndians), 48–52
ancestral tree engraving, 38
anima archetype, 8, 10*f*, 32–34
animals: children's dreams, 121–22, pl. 15; newspaper images, 17–23

anteater (newspaper image), 18, 19*f*
Aphrodite, 93
Aquarius image, 35
archetypal image metaphor, 7
art exhibit: analyst's interest/task, 86; location, 87–89
art exhibit, symbols explored: color, 89; communication barriers, 94–95; compassion for city, 103; death, 100; growth, 93–94; one-sidedness, 99–100; race, 98–99; separation, 101–103; soul food, 97–98; space, 90–91; time and change, 91–93, 95–97; water, 89–90
artists, social role, 84–85
Aztec Indians, 45

baby on bookshelf dream (child's), 116–17, pl. 5
Bachelard, Gaston, 61
back-sack dream (child's), 118–19, pl. 8
bees and statue (newspaper image), 10, 11*f*
birds (newspaper images), 20, 23
Black Elk, 62
black man/gravel path exhibit, 98–99
bleeding dream (child's), 117–18, pl. 7
bluebonnet/cowboy boot towel, 53
brain image metaphor, 7

bread/pewter bed exhibit, 97–98
bridge (newspaper image), 10, 11f

cannibalism archetype, 29
caterpillar (newspaper image), 22f, 23
Catholicism. *See* European explorers
cement/soul metaphor, 92–93
change: and collective unconscious, 6; and reality, xi–xii
child rearing, 50–51, 54–55
children's drawings. *See* drawings; "Dreams in the Classroom"
Christianity. *See* European explorers
church (newspaper image), 10, 11f
circulatory system/trees compared, 76
collective unconscious and change, 6. *See also* newspaper images
College Station visit, 53
color and alchemy, 89
copper plates exhibit, 93–94
corrosion/copper exhibit, 93–94
counter-projection. *See* crossed projection process
cowboy boot/bluebonnet towel, 53
cross (Christian). *See* crucifixion images
crossed projection process: and ancestral psychology, 48–53; and cross/crucifixion symbology, 39, 46–48; European-based, 42–45, 46; Indian-based, 45–46; psychological task of today, 53–57
crucifixion images: symbology of, 46–48; Terena man's dream, 39; trees, 69–70
crying tree, 81, 82f

daguerreotype-based exhibit, 93–94
Daniela (girl), 73–74
death/rebirth dreams (children's), 123–24
depth psychology: ancestral psyche task, 53–57; author's approach, 3, 5–6, 58–61; and education, 106–107; and therapy, 84, 109; urban symbology, 87
Descartes, René, 7
discovery and "New World." *See* Indians (American)
diver-Isis statute (newspaper image), 8, 10f
drawings: author's, 77–79; as expressions of trauma, 72–75; and the unconscious, 78–79. *See also* "Dreams in the Classroom"
dreams: author's, 23, 79; desire for understanding, 24; Jung's layered house, 108; McMillan III's trees, viii; and newspaper images, 24–26, 27–28; Terena man's, 39
"Dreams in the Classroom": animals, 121–22, pl. 15; death/rebirth, 123–24; family/home, 114–16, pl. 1–pl. 4; God, 124, pl. 16; growth, 118–20, pl. 8–pl. 11; heroes, 122–23; project methodology/beginnings, 108–13, 125; school-oriented, 116–18, pl. 5–pl. 7; witches, 120–21, pl. 12–pl. 14
driving dream (child's), 120, pl. 11
drought/geese (newspaper images), 17–18

drug problem, transforming, 91–93
duck dream (child's), 116, pl. 3
Dwelling (exhibit), 90

earthworm dream (child's), 121–22, pl. 15
eclipse (newspaper image), 12, 14
education, one-sided approach, 104–108. *See also* "Dreams in the Classroom"
egocide, defined, 47
ego consciousness. *See* rationality
electrical lines and trees, 58–59, 63–67
elements (newspaper images), 12–17
elephant's tooth (newspaper image), 17
Enchanted Rock visit, viii
Encyclopedia of Psychoanalysis, 106
equator-sin declaration (papal), 42
Ethiopian man, 98–99, 129*n*6
European explorers: as ancestral father, 48–52; ego-centered psyche, 40–41; and Indian projections, 45–46; projections of, 42–45. *See also* Indians (American)
Eve projection, 44

family-oriented dreams (children's), 114–16, pl. 1–pl. 4
father archetype, 48–52, 54–55
feminine archetype, 10, 32–34, 56–57
Fierz, Heinrich Karl, 23, 60
finger dream (child's), 117–18, pl. 7
fire images, 12, 14, 15*f*
fish dream (author's), 23
fish (newspaper image), 23

flag-jewel (newspaper image), 34
flower dream (child's), 114
"flower hands" dream (child's), 120, pl. 10
flying saucer dream (child's), 117, pl. 6
funerary urns image, 8, 9*f*

garbage: dreams/images, 24, 25*f*; and trees, 75–76
Garden of the Shadow, 87–89
geese/drought images, 17–18
God dream (child's), 124, pl. 16
God-satellite comparison, 12
gorilla (newspaper image), 18
gravel path/black man exhibit, 98–99
green light in alchemy, 20
Growth and Guilt (Zoja), 94
growth dreams (children's), 118–20, pl. 8–pl. 11
growth problems and trees, 71–75
Guarani Indians, 45

hands as flowers dream (child's), 120, pl. 10
helicopter (newspaper image), 18, 19*f*
hen dream (child's), 115–16
hero dreams (children's), 111, 117, 122–23
Hillman, James, 87
hippopotamus and ants dream (child's), 122
home-oriented dreams (children's), 114–16, pl. 1–pl. 4
hospital tree, 76
House of Lanterns (exhibit), 90–91

House-Tree-Person test, 72
housing (newspaper image), 20

imagination and education, 105–106
immortality, Talmud description, ix
India, tree sacredness, 75
Indians (American): as ancestral mother, 48–52; ancient cultures, 37–38, 39; consciousness of, 41–42; and cross/crucifixion symbology, 46–48; destruction *vs.* integration, 38–40, 71–72; and European projections, 42–45; modern, 38–39, 55–56; projections onto Europeans, 45–46; psychological task, 53–57; and trees, 79–82
insects (newspaper images), 20–23
intelligence and unconscious, 106–108
Isis statue-diver (newspaper images), 8, 10*f*

Jasone (Terena native), 39
Jesuit missionaries, 44–45
jewelry (newspaper images), 32, 34
joy dreams (children's), 124
Jupiter (newspaper image), 12, 13*f*

Kalff, Dora, 97
Kamayurá Indians, 80–81
Kawai, Hayao, 98
knowledge and unconscious, 106–108

"The Lambspring Figures," 128*n*3
lamp post drawing (author's), 79, 80*f*

Latin American identity, ancestral psyche, 48–52. *See also* Indians (American)
Lenin cake (newspaper image), 29, 31*f*
lightning bug (newspaper image), 20, 21*f*
Louis XIV-politician (newspaper images), 26, 29, 30*f*
Lucifer projections, 43–44

male-female relations (European-Indian), 40, 43–44, 48–52, 54–55
mandala symbolism, 61
McMillan, Frank, III, viii
Memories, Dreams, and Reflections (Jung), 108
mercury, 91–93
messianism (Indian), 45
monkey dream (child's), 122
monsters: children's dreams, 115, 119, 120–21, 123, pl. 9, pl. 12–pl. 14; newspaper images, 8, 10
Moore, Thomas, 62
mother archetype: and Latin American identity, 48–52, 54–55; newspaper image, 18
mummy-actress (newspaper images), 32, 33*f*
myths/mythmaking: newspaper images, 8–11; as soul expressions, 3–4

nest/housing comparison, 20
newspaper images: anima, 32–34; animal world, 17–23; author's hypothesis, xiii, 5–7, 35; dream world, 24–26, 27–28; elements,

12–17; myth-oriented, 8–11; power symbols, 26, 29–32; as psyche medium, 4–5; role of Jungian analysts, 34–36

O Estado de São Paulo, circulation statistics, 5. *See also* newspaper images
oil spill (newspaper image), 23
one-sidedness: art/alchemy metaphor, 99–100; education, 104–108
Oshossi (deity), 59

pacifier dream (child's), 119–20
Palace of Death and Darkness, 91
palm trees, 58–59, 76
Paradise fantasy/projection, 40, 44
parenting, 50–51, 54–55
Peron, Evita (newspaper image), 34
"The Philosophical Tree" (Jung), 61
Pices era, 23, 35
Pinochet (newspaper image), 12, 13*f*
playground dreams (children's), 118
political figures (newspaper images), 8, 12, 13*f*, 26, 29, 30*f*
Portuguese explorers. *See* European explorers
power archetype, 8
power-oriented images, 26, 29–32
presidents (newspaper images), 8, 26, 29, 30*f*
projections. *See* crossed projection process; trees

Quarup ritual, 80–81
Quetzalcoatl projection, 45

Rafael (boy), 74–75
railway ties exhibit, 90
rainbow (newspaper image), 14, 16*f*
rain dream (child's), 115
Ramses statue-secretary of treasury (newspaper images), 8
rationality: education, 105–106; European development, 40–41
reality, challenge of change, xi–xii
rivers/trees compared, 77
Rodrigo (boy), 72–73
Rolls Royce symbol, 32
Rosen, David, 47, 53

sand/hole exhibit, 95–97
sandplay therapy, 97
São Paulo: art exhibits, 86–88; population statistics, 83; tree statistics, 63
sarcophagi (newspaper image), 8, 9*f*
satellite-produced images, 12, 13*f*
school dreams (children's), 116–18, pl. 5–pl. 7
secretary of treasury-Ramses statue (newspaper images), 8
senator-Louis XIV (newspaper images), 26, 29, 30*f*
shamans, 44–45, 79–80
shark dreams (children's), 121–22
shoe exhibit, 99–100
sibling dreams (children's), 122
silo exhibit, 89–90
Sioux Indians, 62
slavery and suicide, 55

spider dream (child's), 116, pl. 4
Spider man-president (newspaper image), 8
sports images, 26
squares exhibit, 94–95
Staden, Hans, 29
suicide and slavery, 55
sun/eclipse (newspaper image), 12, 14
Superman dream (child's), 123
synchronicity, role of, 60–61
syringe/mercury exhibit, 91–93

teachers: in dreams project, 108–13; surrogate mother role, 104–105
therapy, 94, 109
Ticuna painting, 79–80
treeboy myth, 81–82
trees: analyst's interest/task, 58–59, 81–82; biological response to trimming, 69; as garbage receptacles, 75–76; human biology compared, 76–77; McMillan's dream, viii; planting/trimming mutilations, 63–71, 74f; as projections of growth problems, 71–75; rivers compared, 77; sacredness/importance, 62–63, 79–81; symbolism, 61–62, 64, 67, 69–70; synchronicity experience, 60–61
tribal life, 37–38, 39, 55–56
turtles, vii–viii

Umbanda religion, 59
unus mundus, 127n2
urban unconsciousness. *See* art exhibit, symbols explored; trees
von Franz, Marie-Louise, 34, 56
von Martius, Carl, 38

water: in alchemy, 89–90; dreams about, 24; newspaper images, 14, 15f
weed drawing (author's), 78–79
whale dream (child's), 115, pl. 2
wind, newspaper images, 14
witch dreams (children's), 120–21, pl. 12–pl. 14
womb dream (child's), 114, pl. 1
writing skills, "Dreams" project, 111

Xavante Indians, newspaper image, 29, 32

Zoja, Luigi, 94
Zoro Indians, 50–51

Carolyn and Ernest Fay Series in Analytical Psychology
David H. Rosen, General Editor
TEXAS A&M UNIVERSITY PRESS

Beebe, John. *Integrity in Depth*, 1992.

Hollis, James. *The Archetypal Imagination*, 2000.

Kast, Verena. *Joy, Inspiration, Hope*, 1991.

Kawai, Hayao. *Buddhism and the Art of Psychotherapy*, 1996.

Stein, Murray. *Transformation: Emergence of the Self*, 1998.

Stevens, Anthony. *The Two Million-Year-Old Self*, 1993.

Woodman, Marion. *The Stillness Shall Be the Dancing: Feminine and Masculine in Emerging Balance* (audio), 1994.

Young-Eisendrath, Polly. *Gender and Desire: Uncursing Pandora*, 1997.

ISBN 1-58544-214-3